"Six Thousand Truckers Can't Be Wrong"

"Six Thousand Truckers Can't Be Wrong"

Dr. Daniel Joseph Tutty

iUniverse, Inc.
New York Lincoln Shanghai

"Six Thousand Truckers Can't Be Wrong"

iUniverse books may be ordered through booksellers or by contacting:

iUniverse
2021 Pine Lake Road, Suite 100
Lincoln, NE 68512
www.iuniverse.com
1-800-Authors (1-800-288-4677)

ISBN-13: 978-0-595-37685-8 (pbk)
ISBN-13: 978-0-595-82067-2 (ebk)
ISBN-10: 0-595-37685-1 (pbk)
ISBN-10: 0-595-82067-0 (ebk)

Printed in the United States of America

Contents

Acknowledgement

The creative process is a long and sometimes frustrating path. Despite all of the best intentions, the final product is the result of many long hours of monotonous and repetitive iterations and reiterations. The dedication of my wife to this arduous task is testimony to her love and devotion to the individual credited with this body of work. Her level of skill and contribution to this effort are beyond calculation and far surpass my ability to adequately express my eternal appreciation.

Nonetheless, I now acknowledge my love and gratitude to my wife, Kathryn, for her persistence and patience in bringing my life-long ambition to reality. Thanks, my love, for everything.

I cannot engage in this process of acknowledgement without pointing out the mentor whose insight and experience in this process provided the initial focus and direction for this project. It was his encouragement, direction and particularly his patience, which enabled this task to reach a successful conclusion.

I therefore wish to give a special acknowledgement to Dr. Ed Anhalt of Wisconsin. My hope is that this book will represent the start of a long personal and professional association with this esteemed gentleman and outstanding scholar.

Précis

In "Six Thousand Truckers Can't Be Wrong" I trace the development of the world's oldest profession from ancient Samaria to modern day Nevada. I focus primarily on a brand of prostitution, which has been effectively and successfully practiced in the American West. Specifically, I focus on brothel prostitution, which has continuously operated for over one hundred and fifty years in Nevada, the only place in the United States where it is legal.

I conducted research in Elko County, Nevada. Elko County is a vast rural area of 16,000 square miles. There are seven legally operated houses of prostitution. A sample size of one hundred citizens, eighty percent of who were women, responded to the question of whether or not they felt that legalized bordello prostitution should be allowed to continue in Nevada. The majority said yes. In fact the survey indicated that seventy-five percent of those in favor of prostitution identified themselves as members of fundamental churches. Not only were they in favor of legalized prostitution in Nevada, but they also felt it should be legalized across the United States.

In my research I interviewed two sex workers, a house "manager", and two house owners, including the president of the Nevada Brothel Owners Association. I also interviewed representatives of the law enforcement agency responsible for monitoring the activities of these houses.

The results were surprising. The presence of bordello prostitution actually lowers the incidence of violent crime. In fact, in Elko County, Nevada, there was only one case of violent crime associated with prostitution in the past thirteen years.

Since these figures have been kept by the Nevada State Health Department, there has yet to be a single reported case of AIDS among the sex workers or their clients. Further, of the nearly 1,000 sex workers operating in Nevada, the incidence of any reportable sexually transmitted disease is less than one percent. Contrast that with the nearly 15 percent of sexually transmitted diseases for the adolescent female population in Elko County, Nevada.

There are no "streetwalkers" on the streets of Elko. Law enforcement costs are negligible. Contrast this to the costs of law enforcement in New York City where the annual costs to enforce the laws against prostitution can run as high as forty-two million dollars.

But what, you may ask, is the benefit for everyone to be obtained from the operation of bordello prostitution in a community? The answer is money, lots and lots of money.

My research has shown that the "average" sex worker has a net annual income of $160,000. Not bad for a person who works two hours and forty-five minutes a day. Take that figure and consider the following. The sex worker gives 50 percent of her gross earnings to the "house". The federal government takes 40 percent of the gross income. There are 1,000 sex workers in Nevada. Thus, the annual gross income for the sex workers of Nevada is 163 million dollars.

The average sex worker is in the 40 percent tax bracket. Thus, the average income received by the federal government for the operation of legalized prostitution in Nevada is 6.5 million dollars. The population of Nevada is 2.5 million. The population of the United States of America is about 100 times that figure (250 Million). If brothel prostitution were nationally legalized, the potential federal tax revenues annually would amount to 65.2 billion dollars.

Just imagine the number of worthwhile programs that could be funded by that level of annual revenue. The revenue that would be saved from the costs of law enforcement would add even more revenue for such programs.

The average state income tax is around 23 percent of the federal tax. Thus the states and subsequently the county and municipal governments would have about 337 million dollars annually for schools, roads, homeless shelters and property tax relief.

I grant you that more research is needed in the application of essentially a rural population based program to an urban environment. I speak to these issues in the conclusion section of the book. The study of the application of this model to a highly urbanized environment will be the substance of my next book.

My research reveals that an average of six thousand over-the-road truckers frequent a brothel in Wells, Nevada, on a monthly basis. That figure is three times the population of that community. Read the book and learn for yourself that "Six Thousand Truckers Can't Be Wrong."

1

Hypothesis

The major hypothesis for this book centers on the adoption as a model for the entire country of a form of prostitution that has continuously operated quite successfully here in the American West for over two hundred years. Specifically, the type of prostitution I am speaking of is Bordello prostitution, commonly known as "Cat House" prostitution.

Not only will I demonstrate that such a model can be successfully implemented in the rest of the country but I will also point out some of the many positive results of the adoption of this model here in the West. The logical implications for the rest of the country seem obvious. If the model can successfully operate on a small scale here in Nevada, there is no reason to assume that it cannot be just as successfully operated on a national scale.

The adoption of the Nevada Model of Prostitution will have a number of very positive results for the entire country to include:

1. Lower the rate of violent crime

2. Lower the incidence of Sexually Transmitted Disease

3. Significantly lower the costs of law enforcement related to the control of street prostitution

4. Generating huge sums of tax revenues for city, county and state governments

5. Create huge funding sources for much needed municipal projects such as:

    • Shelter for the homeless

    • Community food banks

- Street improvements
- Neighborhood reclamation projects
- School construction
- Teacher salaries
- Municipal workers' salaries
- Improved emergency medical services

6. Eliminate "streetwalkers" from our communities

7. Reduce the influence of organized crime in the Prostitution industry

The reason I know that the Nevada Model can work for the rest of the country is simply because it already works in Nevada. Prostitution is strictly regulated in Nevada (see Appendix 1, Nevada Statutes). However, accepting the reality of human nature, the legislators of this State provided for the legal provision of this service. This service provision is highly structured and monitored constantly (the Nevada Model).

What is the Nevada Model? Simply stated, the Nevada Model allows for the operation of Houses of Prostitution in areas of population under 400,000, provided the voters of that political structure give majority consent. Brothel owners submit an application to the city or county government for a permit to operate as a private business within the legal jurisdiction of that political structure. If all health and environmental requirements are met and a background check is passed by the owner, then a business license is issued for one year. This license is subject to annual renewal and may be revoked for any major health, environmental or legal violation. The annual fee is $1,500. All of the sex workers in a particular house must have weekly check-ups by a licensed physician for the presence of any sexually transmitted disease. If she fails this examination, her work permit is revoked. She must also pass a monthly general health exam to avoid the possible spread of any infectious or communicable diseases.

The workers are subject to Federal Taxation laws as independent contractors. They therefore must report all income on Form 1099 on their annual IRS income tax report.

The workers are also restricted after 5:00 P.M. to remain in residence at the place of employment until 8:00 A.M. of the following day. If there is a necessity to be out of the residence during those hours, the workers must notify law enforcement and obtain prior approval by the local law enforcement agency. If this is not done, and a worker is found in violation, the law enforcement agency will revoke that individual's work permit. (Appendices 1 and 3)

The houses are not allowed to advertise in any fashion as a House of Prostitution and therefore are listed as men's clubs or bars. As such, the house must obtain a liquor license as well as an occupancy permit. (Appendix 3, 4) As a result of these regulations, there are no streetwalkers on the streets of our community. In fact, unless a person is seeking such services, the presence of the "houses" goes unnoticed by the average citizen. At one time in the early 1990's in Elko, Nevada, a local church was located within three blocks of the local houses and there was never any dissention among the church members.

Why should the rest of the country adopt the Nevada Model? One need only look at a few statistics related to prostitution and the reasons become clear.

"Prostitution is defined as the performance of sexual acts solely for the purpose of material gain." (1) Persons prostitute themselves when they grant sexual favors to others in exchange for money, gifts or other payments and in so doing use their bodies as commodities. In legal terms, the word prostitute refers only to those who engage overtly in such sexual-economic transactions, usually for a specified sum of money. (Appendix 1)

Prostitution is an act of violence against women, which is intrinsically traumatizing. In a study of 475 people in prostitution (including women, men and the trans gendered) from five countries, South Africa, Thailand, Turkey, the U.S.A, and Zambia the following was reported:

- 62% reported having been raped
- 73% reported physical assault
- 72% were currently or formerly homeless
- 67% met the criteria for Post Traumatic Stress Disorder
- 92% stated they wanted to escape prostitution immediately (29)

Prostitutes may be of either sex, but throughout history the majority have been women, reflecting both traditional socioeconomic dependence of women and the tendency to exploit female sexuality. Although Prostitution has often been characterized as the "world's oldest profession" the concept of women as property, which prevailed in most cultures until the end of the 19th.Century, meant that the profits of the profession most often accrued to the men who controlled it. (29)

Men have traditionally been characterized as procurers and customers, but they are increasingly being identified as prostitutes. They generally serve male customers and sometimes impersonate women. (1) The average age of entry into prostitution is thirteen. Estimates of the prevalence of incest among prostitutes range from 65 to 90 per cent.

The Council for Prostitution Alternatives of Portland, Oregon in its 1991 Annual Report stated that 85% of prostitutes/clients reported a history of sexual abuse in childhood; 70% reported incest. (13) The United Nations estimates that four million people a year are trafficked in prostitution. Centered in Moscow and Kiev, the crime networks run women to Japan and Thailand, where thousands of young Slavic women are used against their wills as prostitutes. Russian crime groups in Moscow control the routes. Seeking a better life, the women are lured by local advertisements for good jobs in foreign countries at wages they could never imagine at home.

Estimates from the Ukraine number as high as 400,000 women under the age of 30 have left their homeland for the life of a prostitute in the past ten years. The Thai Embassy in Moscow receives nearly 1,000 visa applications a day. In Israel prostitution is not illegal, but brothels are. In that country there are 250,000 foreign male workers. Most are single men or married men living there without their wives.

Police estimate that there are 25,000 paid sexual transactions every day. Brothels are ubiquitous. Women are held in apartments where each woman services as many as fifteen clients per day. In

Israel, among other countries, there is not even a specific law against the sale of human beings. In Istanbul, Turkey, two women were thrown to their deaths from a balcony while six of their friends watched. In Serbia, a young Ukrainian woman who refused to work as a prostitute was beheaded in public. In Milan, Italy, a week before Christmas, police broke up a ring that was holding auctions in which women abducted from countries in the former Soviet Union were put on blocks, partially naked, and sold at an average price of just under $1,000. (29)

"This is happening everywhere you look." said Michael Platzer, the Vienna, Austria-based Head of Operations for the United Nation's Center for International Crime Prevention. "The Mafia is not stupid. There is less law enforcement since the Soviet Union fell apart and there is more freedom of movement. The earnings are incredible. The overhead is low. You don't have to buy cars and guns. Drugs you sell once and they are gone. Women can earn money for a long time." (21)

Until the 1960's, attitudes toward prostitutes were based on the Judeo-Christian view of morality. Recent research has attempted to separate moral issues from the reality of prostitution. (8) The rationale for its continued illegal status in the United States of America rests on three assumptions:

- Prostitution is linked to organized crime
- Prostitution is responsible for much ancillary crime
- Prostitution is the cause of an increase in sexually transmitted disease

These assumptions are now in question. Recognized experts have pointed out that prostitution is no longer an attractive investment for organized crime because it is difficult to control, is too visible, and affords to small a return compared to the severe penalties for procurement.

It is obvious that ancillary crime such as larceny, robbery, assault and misuse of narcotics does occur in conjunction with prostitution. This is especially true when a streetwalker is involved. Whether it is rational to make one activity criminal in order to reduce or control another merits serious inquiry.

Finally, public health officials indicate that prostitutes account for only a small percentage of the sexually transmitted disease cases in the United States of America. Greater sexual freedom has made young people the major source of such cases. (3)

Furthermore, strong arguments have been made in support of legalizing prostitution. Decriminalization would free courts and police from handling victimless crime, allowing law enforcement more time to deal with serious and violent crimes.

The constitutional question of violation of equal protection has been raised, since the law penalizes prostitutes but not their customers. Polls have shown that about half of the United States of America population would favor decriminalization of prostitution throughout the country. (8) In order to understand the necessity for change in the United States of America in the manner that prostitution is handled we must first examine the day-to-day reality of prostitution, United States style.

Consider the following:

- In the United States there are over 100,00 arrests per year for prostitution
- There are over one million people in the United States that have worked as prostitutes. This equals 1% of all American women.
- The average prostitution arrest is 70% female sex worker, 20% male sex worker and 10% customer.
- 90% of the women arrested for prostitution are women of color
- Street prostitution is 10–20% of the total for large cities such as Los Angeles, San Francisco and New York.
- In smaller cities, the percentages for street prostitution are as high as 50%.
- 30% of the prostitutes in larger cities, such as San Francisco, are male.
- 25% of the female prostitutes are transgender. (29)

Consider the impact prostitution has in terms of other areas. In the area of substance abuse studies in the United States of America there were found a prevalence of substance abuse and addiction ranging up to 84% for the industry. Substance abuse is relatively common among street prostitutes (about 50%) but is rare among women who work off the street. One study showed that nearly 50% of the population of women who used drugs did so before becoming prostitutes. (14)

The United States Department of Health consistently reports only 3–5% of sexually transmitted diseases in this country are related to prostitution, compared to 35% among teenagers. (12) There is no statistical indication in the United

States population that prostitutes are vectors of H.I.V., although a small percentage of prostitutes may be H.I.V. positive. (14)

Violence is a major problem for women and prostitutes. One study reported that 83% of prostitutes are victims of assault with a weapon. (14) A Canadian Report on Prostitution and Pornography concluded that girls and women in prostitution have a mortality rate 40 times higher than the national average. (14) In one study, 75% of women in escort prostitution had attempted suicide. Prostituted women comprised 15% of all completed suicides reported by hospitals. Figures vary. (29)

According to one massage parlor owner, over 90% of abuse against some prostitutes takes place within domestic relationships. Between 35 and 85 percent of prostitutes are survivors of early sexual abuse. (1) A study of 130 streetwalkers (primarily homeless) who engaged in survival sex or prostitution found that 80% had been physically assaulted. Some prostitutes are raped between eight and ten times a year. Of those raped, 7% seek help from a rape crisis center and only 4% report the rape to the police. (8) A recent study showed that in cases of non-domestic rape and abuse, 5% of the perpetrators identified themselves as police officers. They often would produce badges and police identifications. This does not include actual cases of police misconduct and rape. (8)

Although violence is a serious problem, some populations of prostitutes show no higher incidence of violence and abuse than women in general. (11) Some researchers suggest that prostitutes, in general, suffer from "negative identities" or lack of "self-esteem". A 1986 study by Diane Prince however, found call girls and brothel workers had higher self-esteem than before they were prostitutes. 97% of the call girls sampled liked themselves "more than before".

This study also examined suicide rates and is often misquoted, referring to a statistic regarding "call girls". In the context of pathologizing prostitutes, some mistakenly report that 75% of call girls have attempted suicide. However, according to this study, 76% of call girls considered (not attempted) suicide, (along with 61% of non-prostitutes) and only 42% of brothel workers. (29) Although little research has been done regarding client profiles, anecdotal reports and arrest statistics indicate that clients vary widely in terms of race and class. In a study in London, England, 50% of clients were married or cohabitating. According to Kinsey's report, 70% of adult men have engaged in prostitution at least once.

Male prostitutes sometimes report that their clients include married men who identify as heterosexual.

Customers are rarely arrested more than once for prostitution and are infrequently jailed. "Police officers arrest prostitutes for "public nuisance" or "loitering" violations or by disguising themselves as customers. They will approach someone they suspect of prostitution, and solicit their services until this person is deceived into agreeing to perform sex for money. The individual is then arrested for offering or agreeing to an act of prostitution. Arrests of prostitution necessarily include the use of entrapment, an invasion of privacy, and/or the use of discriminatory laws or tactics. The average arrest, court and incarceration costs amount to nearly $2,000 per arrest. Cities spend an average of $7.5 million on prostitution control every year, ranging from 1 million dollars (Memphis, Tennessee) to 23 million dollars (New York)(29)

The purpose of this book is essentially to present a logical application of a system which has successfully operated in Nevada for over two hundred years. Prostitution is a timeless institution and the legal sanctioning of bordello prostitution goes back to the time of the ancient Greeks. Mankind will seek sexual services, whether it is legalized or not. One need only look at the horrors associated with prostitution to know that there must be a change.

"During four centuries, 12 million people were believed to be involved in the slave trade between Africa and the New World.

The 200 million—and many of course are women who are trafficked for sex—is a current figure. It's happening now, today". (New York Times, Sunday, January 11,1998.)

Nevada is unique in the United States regarding the legal operation of brothel prostitution. Nevada Law, passed in 1971 allows rural counties the option of legalizing brothels. (Appendix 1) The Nevada statutes clearly show a fairly typical legal response to the issue of prostitution. This is a response that the other forty-nine States have also made. But Nevada has also developed a unique method of dealing with this issue. Has this more enlightened response been considered elsewhere? The answer is yes.

Let us consider the case of the Netherlands. Brothels were illegal in the Netherlands by the law of 1912. What happened to change this situation? During the time since 1912 the government of the Netherlands reached several conclusions:

- The laws against brothels were not enforced
- Efforts at enforcement proved ineffectual
- The costs of litigation were prohibitive and ineffectual in reducing the incidence of prostitution

After studying the issues, the government of the Netherlands decided to adopt a new legal policy regarding prostitution, which went into effect on September 1, 2000.

The reasons for the new law were the following:

- End the abuses in the sex industry
- The Netherlands wants the law to reflect everyday reality
- Prevent prostitute exploitation
- Have more governmental control over the sex industry and counter abuses
- Institute firmer actions against offenders
- Protect the interests of prostitutes themselves
- Facilitate action against sexual violence and abuse and the traffic in persons

The new law, known as Article 250A of the Criminal Code reflects the following policy.

- The employment of prostitution is regulated by municipal licenses. The municipal authorities set rules for brothels operating within their jurisdiction.
- They are authorized to publish bylaws governing their establishment, the premises in which they operate, and the way they are run, using as a guideline a model drafted by the Association of Netherlands Municipalities.
- Regulations on premises specify the minimum size of working areas and govern safety, fire precautions, and hygiene.

For example, every working area must have hot and cold running water; and, must provide condoms. Regulations on the operation of brothels govern the position and status of prostitutes, protecting their physical and mental integrity and prohibiting the employment of minors or people without a valid residence permit. There are also measures to prevent excessive nuisance in neighborhoods where brothels are located.

The local authorities may grant a license to all brothels that conform to all applicable regulations. Specifically Article 250A states:

- It is not illegal to engage in prostitution
- Employed prostitutes must be over 17 years of age and do the work voluntarily
- It is a criminal offense to traffic in persons
- It is a criminal offense to force another person to engage in prostitution or to involve a minor in Prostitution. (The maximum penalty is 8 Years in prison)
- It is not an offense to operate a brothel
- It is illegal to force another person to engage in prostitution including a minor to engage in prostitution
- It is illegal to recruit, abduct or take a person to engage in prostitution in another country (pursuant to the 1933 International Convention for the Suppression of the Traffic in Women of Full Age).
- It is illegal to receive income from prostitution involving a minor or a person forced to engage in prostitution
- It is illegal to force another person to surrender income from prostitution

Today, most countries around the Netherlands pursue a similar course. In 1949 the United Nations adopted a resolution in favor of decriminalization of prostitution. The resolution was ratified by fifty countries and excluded the United States of America. Many countries complied by decriminalizing prostitution, per se, leaving all related activities criminal such as soliciting, advertising, etc. In 1973 the National Organization for Women passed a resolution supporting the decriminalization of prostitution. (13)

An article that appeared in USA TODAY on November 5, 2003, titled "In Belgium, brothels are big business" further discusses the European perspective on this issue. Noelle Knox put the article together. She is on the USA TODAY staff.

Ghent, Belgium-Bridgette doesn't worry about getting arrested because she is a prostitute. She worries about the police because she runs a brothel. That isn't legal, at least not yet. Bridgette (who asked that her real name not be used) ducks the law by calling her brothel a massage parlor. "I am the one who gives them permission to prostitute themselves. And so, under the law in Belgium, I am a pimp," she says. A veteran of eighteen years in the sex business, Bridgette wants brothels to be legalized. However, she is skeptical any politician will push through legislation. But Belgium's new prime minister, Guy Verhostadt, has made legalizing bordellos one of his government's goals. Faced with the reality of brothels and the Europe-wide problems that come with them-human trafficking, drugs and sexually transmitted diseases-the year Belgian parliament is expected to pass a law next year.

Three bills in favor have been introduced in both houses of parliament. "I am certain there will be a law," says Hilde Vautmans, a member of Belgium's parliament, who favors legalizing bordellos". I don't know how much time (it will take) but I think the minds of the people in the parties now in government are really in favor of it." The proposals are patterned after laws "passed in the Netherlands and Germany. In Belgium, the bills would give prostitutes the same legal rights as any employee or self-employed person. The women and men working in the sex trade would have to pay taxes (the government estimates it could take in $55 million a year.) They would be eligible to receive social security and health care benefits.

The brothel owners also would be licensed and required to prove their prostitutes are in the country legally and have work permits. By requiring prostitutes to register, the government will be able to dictate safe-sex standards and better working conditions. A competing proposal against bordellos follows Sweden's model, which not only outlaws prostitution, but also penalizes customers with fines or six months in prison. "I fully disagree (with plans to legalize brothels), and a lot of women's groups disagree with that proposed legislation," says Anne-Marie Lizin, a member of parliament who has co-sponsored the bill against brothels and their customers. "You cannot say you're fighting the trafficking of people and at the same time legalize (brothels) because you open the market."

The debate over changing Belgium's law will likely spread far beyond Belgium, which hosts the headquarters of the 15-member European Union and the North Atlantic Treaty Organization, the U.S.-backed military alliance.

Walking around the red light districts in Belgian cities, it's hard to believe bordellos are outlawed here. Dozens of boutique-style brothels with large front windows line the streets set aside by politicians for prostitution. What's for sale is on display: women dressed in lingerie and stiletto heels. The brothels claim to be bars or clubs with sexy waitresses who serve beer, champagne and soft drinks.

But the prostitutes pay the bar owner about $120 to rent window space for eight hours. When a customer enters, she draws her curtains and charges about $55 for sex. About 80,000 people visit prostitutes in Belgium each day, according to an official government estimate. That's more than the daily number who go to the movies, says Jean-Marie Dedecker, a member of parliament. According to official reports, the Belgian capital of Brussels has become a center for the trade of children in prostitution. The problem, Dedecker says, is not the existence of the sex trade, but the problems that go with it. About two-thirds of Belgium's estimated 10,000 prostitutes were brought in illegally by pimps from eastern European countries such as Russia. Others enter from Africa. It can be big business for organized crime and even some governmental officials.

Three thousand women came into Belgium from Nigeria alone in the past five or six years, says Dedecker, who sits on the government's co mission on human trafficking. "The Nigerian embassy helps to falsify their passports. After petrol, the biggest export of Nigeria is people." "The Europeans have a more liberal attitude toward paid sex and a more liberal attitude toward nudity," says Richard Posner, a judge for the 7th Circuit Court of Appeals in Chicago and co-author of A Guide to America's Sex Laws. He adds, "I don't think there's much of a perceived crisis in dealing with prostitution problems (in the U.S.A.). There are so many other concerns on (politicians') menus, I don't think there is pressure to change these laws."

And, while illegal immigration is a problem in the United States of America, it is less often linked to human trafficking in the sex-for-sale world where girls are lured from foreign countries and forced to be prostitutes. Still, the problem of trafficking of people for the sex trade recently has become an important issue for the United States at home and abroad. In his address to the United Nations in September, 2003, President George W. Bush called for a global effort to stop human trafficking. He said 800,000 to 900,000 people are bought, sold, or forced across borders, many of them teenage girls, some as young as 5 years old, destined for the sex industry. This issue is significant to evangelical Christians, who are some of Bush's most-loyal supporters. "The victims of sex trade see little of life before they see the very worst of life: an underground of brutality and lonely fear," Bush told the U.N. General Assembly.

The State Department estimates 18,000–20,000 people are trafficked into the USA each year, although not necessarily for the sex trade. The United States enacted a law in 2000 to ensure traffickers are punished, victims are protected and government agencies take action. The State Department, which views such trafficking as a human rights issue, produces an annual report on countries' efforts—or failure—to end the practice. In its 2003 report, the State Department suggests that countries that don't make efforts to end human trafficking could face sanctions.

While Belgium pro-legalization plans are following the lead of the Netherlands and Germany, the new laws in those countries have produced mixed results. Brothels were legalized in Holland three years ago. But many local governments are still trying to implement the law. Some businesses-banks, for example-continue to discriminate against sex workers by refusing to let the women open accounts. Problems with tax evasion and illegal immigrants are rampant. Only 5%-10% of the estimated 20,000 prostitutes in the Netherlands pay taxes, according to Mariska Majoor, a former sex worker who now heads the Prostitution Information Centre in Amsterdam. "Tax people work very hard, but they don't work very hard on the street," she says.

Many prostitutes also cannot register with the government to work as prostitutes because they come from countries such as Russia and Albania, which are not part of the 15-nation European Union. Since brothels were legalized in the Netherlands, these women have become street prostitutes. Though it is more dangerous, the women would rather sell their bodies on street corners than return to impoverished conditions in their home countries, Majoor say. "There is a little bit of a panic situation among the illegal and migrant prostitutes because they don't know where to go but the streets," Majoor says.

For many women operating under the police radar, the situation will improve next year when the European Union adds 10 more members, including Poland, Hungary and the Czech Republic. Women from these countries will be eligible to apply for work permits in any EU country. Germany, which legalized brothels in January 2002, also is struggling to implement the law. Many prostitutes don't want to register because they will have to pay income taxes for prior years. Government agencies declined to provide figures for how much tax has been collected from prostitutes.

"We wish the effect (of the law) was bigger" in terms of taxes, concedes Kathrin Bauer, a spokes-woman for women's policies of the Green political party in Germany. Belgian politicians and prostitutes know ending the ban on brothels won't be easy. The reasons women turn to prostitution are complicated. Pimps, who often double as traffickers, usually lure younger women. Older women may be desperate for money. Drugs often fuel their motives. The solutions are controversial, and the debates are passionate.

Bridgette says she has conflicted feelings about the sex trade. She has testified at government hearings in favor of legalizing bordellos and still services a handful of long-time clients. Yet she admits prostitution "kills you." Her story is unusual because she turned to prostitution at the age of 41, after her clothing boutique went out of business and she lost her home trying to pay off debts. After working in a "club" for six years, she had enough money to buy a home in an industrial suburb of Ghent, 30 miles northwest of Brussels. She turned it into a brothel and now has four girls working for her. The gardens are beautifully manicured and the waiting room has pictures of her children and grandchildren.

There are three bedrooms, two of which are specially equipped for sadomasochistic sex. "I am not a woman who can say I hate men. It's not hate. But I cannot have respect anymore for a man, and that's because of the things I've seen," says Bridgette, now 59. Asked if prostitution should exist, Bridgette says no. "But that's because I know there are a lot of women suffering in that business," she says in a voice raw from years of smoking. "For me, even though I'm making good money, it should not exist. But I am a realist and know it's impossible." (13)

The purpose of this book is to promote the use of legalized bordello prostitution across the United States. Once adopted, this system would impact our society in several very favorable ways. Like the system in the Netherlands, the U.S. system would end the abuses in the sex industry. It would reflect the everyday reality of this country. It would increase the level of governmental control over the sex industry. It would significantly reduce the costs of enforcement at all levels of government.

It would enhance the level of tax revenues which could then be channeled into much needed areas of social services such as shelters for the homeless or health care reform. It would reduce the level of violent crime, such as rape. It would reduce the incidence of sexually transmitted diseases. This system, on a small scale in the State of Nevada, has proven very beneficial in many ways for the past thirty-two years. I contend that a thirty year test trial is more than sufficient to indicate the efficacy of this system; and unquestionably signals a plan whose time has come to effectively and efficiently deal with this timeless aspect of the human condition. It is not an effort to legislate the morality of this country but simply reflects the morality of this country.

The recent ruling by the United States Supreme Court of June 26, 2003, which legalized sodomy between two consenting adults has, in fact, established a legal precedent for the morality of this country. Bordello prostitution, like sodomy, is essentially sex between two consenting adults. How can anyone argue the morality of a system that parallels a system that has been sanctioned by the United States Supreme Court? In order to assess the efficacy of Bordello Prostitution in Nevada, we must look at its historical development as well as the historical development of prostitution in general.

2

Historical Development

Prostitution has been a part of human society since the time of the Sumerian Empire (2000 B. C.). Prostitutes were considered to be a temporary wife. Down through the ages the act of sex in exchange for money has been a simple way of life. Greek mythology had Aphrodite, the goddess of love. Temple prostitutes enjoyed positions of honor. Some were even sacrificed to the gods.

In 19th-century Europe the police would seldom enforce anti-prostitution laws. Many of the members of the royal families of Europe enjoyed the company a mistress. The Victorian age in England temporarily halted prostitution. In Puritanical America prostitution, as well as any form of entertainment, was considered frivolous. This attitude forced prostitution to be conducted in secret, except in some more liberal states or territories where the attitude was more tolerant. (25)

Manifest Destiny pushed the United States to the West. Along with the movement of men seeking gold, land and fortune went the world's oldest profession. (5) In the American West of the 1840's there were 50 men for each woman. The first women to arrive were those of easy virtue who came west for the same reasons as the men. (12)

The "red light district" became the social center for many western towns. The term "red light district" is attributed to Dodge City, Kansas. There, the railroaders would hang their red lanterns outside of the "house" during their enjoyment of the ladies. It was not long before the madams realized that hanging a red lantern outside the house was good for business. (27)

Prostitutes provided more than sexual services. In a way they were a surrogate wife or nurse. Prostitutes were one of the most powerful civilizing agents in a rough and tough male-dominated society. (25) The West of the 1850's saw the arrival of "respectable" women. This movement brought churches and the attempt to reform the ladies of easy virtue. This attempt failed due to indifference from the citizenry to the plight of the prostitutes as well as direct opposition by the ladies of the night. The reform movement did have an impact on the profession. Many of the prostitutes moved out of the respectful areas and away from the concern of law. (5) Some moved to less civilized areas such as the territory of Nevada. (25,26)

"Prostitution in various forms has existed from the dawn of time. It is dependent on the economic, social and sexual values of a society. It has been secular or under the guise of religion. In some societies prostitution was believed to ensure the preservation of the family. Women have usually entered prostitution through coercion or under economic stress. In most societies prostitutes have had low social status and a restricted future. Because their sexual service was disapproved and considered degrading, a few female prostitutes, however, have acquired wealth and power through marriage. One example is the Byzantine empress Theodora, wife of Justinian I. (25)

In pre-industrial societies prostitution was widespread. The exchange of wives by their husbands was a practice among many primitive peoples. In the ancient Middle East and India, temples maintained large numbers of prostitutes. Sexual intercourse with them was believed to facilitate communion with the gods. (5)

In ancient Greece, prostitution flourished on all levels of society. Prostitutes of the lowest level worked in licensed brothels and were required to wear distinctive clothing as a badge of their vocation.

Prostitutes of a higher level usually were skilled dancers and singers. Those of the highest level, the "hetaerae", kept salons where politicians met, and they often attained power and influence. In ancient Rome prostitution was common despite severe legal restrictions. Female slaves, captured abroad by the Roman legions, were impressed into urban brothels or exploited by owners in the households they served. The Roman authorities attempted to limit the spread of slave prostitution and often resorted to harsh measures. Brothel inmates, called "meretrices", were forced to register with the government for life, to wear blond wigs and other distinctive clothing, to forfeit all civil rights, and to pay a heavy tax.

In the Middle Ages the Christian Church, which valued chastity, attempted to convert or rehabilitate individual prostitutes but refrained from campaigning against the institution itself. In so doing, the church followed the teaching of St. Augustine, who held that the elimination of prostitution would breed even worse forms of immorality and perversion, because men would continue to seek sexual contact outside of marriage. How prophetic he was!

By the late Middle Ages, prostitution had reached a highpoint in Western history. Licensed brothels flourished throughout Europe, yielding enormous revenues to government officials and corrupt churchmen. In Asia, where women were held in low esteem and no religious deterrent existed, prostitution was accepted as natural.

Prostitution declined sharply in Europe during the sixteenth century, largely as a result of stern reprisals by Protestants and Roman Catholics. They condemned the immorality of brothels and their inmates, but they were also motivated by the perception of a connection between prostitution and an outbreak of syphilis, a previously unknown disease. The authorities closed brothels in many cities. Under a typical ordinance, enacted in Paris in 1635, prostitutes were flogged, shaved bald, and exiled for life without formal trial. (23) These harsh measures did not, however, eradicate prostitution and sexually transmitted disease. Gradually it became obvious that these ills were increasing, especially in the large, crowded cities that accompanied the industrialization of the West in the 18th and 19th Centuries.

Beginning with Prussia in 1700, most continental European governments shifted their tactics from suppression of prostitution and sexually transmitted disease to control through a system of compulsory registration, licensed brothels and medical inspection of prostitutes. Britain, although it did not license brothels, passed Contagious Disease Prevention acts in the 1860's providing for medical inspection of prostitutes in certain naval and military districts. In Britain and the United States, prostitution flourished openly in urban red-light districts. City officials, viewing prostitutes as a "necessary evil", allowed prostitutes to ply their trade as long as they refrained from annoying "respectable" people who happened in the area. A lucrative white-slave trade developed, in which women and girls were shipped across international borders for immoral purposes. (5)

In time the ineffectuality and corruption of licensed prostitution stirred protests throughout Europe. Britain repealed the Contagious Disease Prevention acts, which were not proving to be a deterrent to sexually transmitted disease and were, moreover, regarded as a threat to the civil liberties of their subjects. Many governments sought to check prostitution by attacking the international traffic in women and children. Britain passed the Criminal Amendment Act of 1885 forbidding such traffic and thirteen major powers signed a treaty in 1904 outlawing it and providing for an international exchange of data on the subject. (22) Prostitution in the United States was essentially unchecked until 1910. At that time religious and civic organizations developed a nationwide campaign against both the immorality of prostitution and its relationship to sexually transmitted diseases.

On the federal level, Congress passed the White Slave Traffic Act (the Mann Act) of 1910 forbidding the interstate transport of women and girls for immoral purposes. (3) On the local level, many anti-prostitution laws were passed. Some laws reflected the belief that prostitutes were misguided, coerced unfortunates who needed rehabilitation and protection from procurers. Others represented the view that prostitutes were morally or mentally inferior human beings. Although both kinds of laws still exist, the latter type is enforced today. (4)

Prostitution in the United States today takes various forms, but the majority are the "streetwalkers". These prostitutes solicit or are solicited by customers on city streets for survival. Increasing numbers are young runaways to the city who turn to the streets for survival. Because the statutes are enforced in such a way as to punish overt and visible acts rather than any specific act, almost all of the prostitutes arrested each year are streetwalkers. Customers, although legally culpable, are rarely arrested. (11)

Prostitution in Nevada dates to the 1850's. Brothels were in operation in the mining camps such as Virginia City prior to Nevada becoming a territory of the U.S. in 1861. Prostitution there was as much a part of everyday life as a pick and shovel. The prostitutes were not socially acceptable and were denied protection under the law due to their occupation. Nevada Territory attracted a huge influx of men with the discovery of Silver at the Comstock Load near Virginia City. (26)

One of the more celebrated incidents involved a legendary prostitute in Virginia City named Julie Bulette, known as the prostitute with a heart of gold. On January 20, 1867, the legendary Julia Bulette's dead body was found in her home. She was lying on her left side with her feet halfway out of bed. Sometime during the night she was strangled, shot, suffocated and severely beaten. The Press called her murder atrocious and wrote that it was "outrageous and cruel".

Several months after Julia's funeral, the law arrested John Millian, a French drifter, who claimed he had not murdered her, but said he knew it was going to happen. Due to the town's hatred for Millian, a jury was very difficult to select. The officials couldn't find twelve men who were unbiased and women in 1868 were not allowed to vote. A jury, however, was initially chosen and the accused man was found guilty. He was condemned to die by hanging. At dawn, on April 27, 1868, John Millian met his fate.

The hanging became a spectator event, with everyone hoping to catch a glimpse of the murderer. Excited people came by stage, horseback or on foot from the nearby towns. All of the saloons were closed for only the second time in the history of Virginia City; the first was the day of Julia's funeral. Forty deputies and the National Guard, in full uniform, escorted the carriage carrying Millian and Father Monogue, a priest of St. Mary's Catholic Church.

The physician's vehicle followed the prisoner, and behind it came the news media and a coffin draped in black accompanied by the undertaker and his assistants. The gallows were already in place and several thousand people gathered. The prisoner spoke a few words of French, contending he didn't understand English well enough to defend himself. He kissed the priest, mounted the scaffold, and within two minutes was declared dead. The murder of Julia Bulette was avenged. The crowd returned to Virginia City, opened the saloons and celebrated.

Throughout the entire event, Julia was never referred to as a woman of easy virtue. It was obvious the people finally accepted the goodness in her, despite her profession. (26) In fact, Julia represented an interesting fact. Madams made a significant financial contribution to the economy of the West.

Houses of prostitution employed the largest group of women in the frontier. They also provided a home for thousands of women who would have otherwise been homeless. Most madams acquired their own real estate and provided considerable revenue for the city through property, school and county taxes. They also paid licensing fees and lined the pockets of corrupt police officers and city officials. The local churches and charities also benefited from contributions made by the madams. The local merchants profited from overcharging for the liquor, food and personal goods used by the "house". (27) The significance of the house in extended to the operation of the government. For example, in 1853 with Washington becoming the territory, its first legislative session was held in Madame Damnable's House in Seattle. (18)

The life of the prostitute in Nevada was a life of loneliness. Not only the prostitute, but also her children were considered social outcasts. The female children followed their mothers' career path. The girls were illiterate and working in the profession at an early age.

They were usually alcoholic and drug addicted by their mid-20s.

They were the object of violence, as evidenced by this July 7, 1876, Rocky Mountain News story (31) regarding the life of two young girls who were used as prostitutes. "A beastly woman was before Justice Whitemore yesterday on a charge of harboring young girls for immoral purposes, and the evidence, which is unfit to print, showed that the woman, as well as the males associated with her in this wicked business deserve to be lynched. The men had not yet been arrested. The woman, who gave her named as Mary Gallagan, but who is also known as "Adobe Moll", was committed for trial at the District Court, the crime being beyond the jurisdiction of Justice. One of the two girls decoyed into Moll's den was a little colored girl who some years since lost both her arms by being run over by the cars. She's about 13 years old, and her companion, a white girl, is only 11."

All of the "Soiled Doves" (23) knew their careers were short-lived and few, if any, made plans for a better future. Some became so tired of being abused by men that they turned to another woman for tenderness and or love. Those who once believed the life of a fancy lady would be filled with thrills and excitement found themselves, instead, looking at a foreboding, barren future. Many became so tired of being victimized, that they took it upon themselves to end it by suicide.

One of these sad stories was that of Lottie Ables Pickett. She worked many years in the mining towns in Montana. She came to Helena, Montana, in the 1870's. Her nickname was "Sorrell Mike" after a racehorse she had purchased. She was said to be an attractive dancer with dark auburn hair and gentle manners. She made several suicide attempts. On July 31, 1880, the Butte Daily Miner (7) reported: "Sorrell Mike made up her mind the other day to go and be an angel, and with that intent, swallowed an overdose of morphine". Lottie was an object of ridicule. It was not long after the story appeared in the paper that Lottie was found at home by her sister, laying on the floor with a bullet in her abdomen. At first Lottie claimed that she had been shot by a man. Later, when she knew death was near, she admitted that she had pulled the trigger. The newspaper reported Lottie's age being thirty years old; other records show her to be only 22 at the time of her death. (7)

There are many stories similar to the one of Lottie. The West of 1870's was characterized by many of these types of tragic lives. By far the most tragic of all existences was that of the Chinese prostitute in San Francisco. (9) Purchased in China by wealthy merchants, the girls were then shipped over to the United States. On the voyage they were "trained" by the Captain and crew on the art of pleasing men. The girls were usually around 11 years old. Upon arrival, the girls would be taken to a large cave known as the "Queen's Room."

Older Chinese women further trained them. These women had survived the ordeal of Prostitution. Once the training was completed, the girls would be taken to an auction to be sold. Upon arrival at the auction house, the girls were physically inspected by the potential buyers. This meant that one by one the girls would be stripped and examined. In order to make the sale legal, the given price in gold or currency was placed in the hand of the girl. She would immediately hand the money to the man who had offered her for sale. She was forced to sign a contract, which typically looked like the following:

For the consideration of _____ paid into my hands on this day, I, _____, agree to prostitute my body for the term of ____years.
If, in that time, I am sick one day, two weeks shall be added to my time, and if more than one, my term of prostitution shall be continued an additional month. But, if I run away, or escape from the custody of my keepers, then I am to be held a slave for life:
Signed_____(3)

Of course, any time lost during pregnancies or during monthly menstrual cycles was considered a sick day. Therefore, there was a high probability that a girl would never escape her contract. She would remain the profession until she died of a disease, which usually effected about 90% of the girls, or until they were too old and unattractive to work in the profession. In the 1850's the girls usually sold for a few hundred dollars each. As their popularity increased, the price went even higher.

By the 1890's one-year-old Chinese girls sold upon arrival in San Francisco for $100 each. There were two classes of Chinese prostitutes. The lucky girls were sent to brothels where they enjoyed a certain measure of dignity. They received baths every day. They were known for their cleanliness. They were well fed. They could expect to live around twenty years in the profession before disease would kill them. The lower-class level was a living nightmare. These girls were sent to work in the "crib".

The crib was a term that referred to a rat-infested two-room operation in China Town. There the girls were placed six in a room. They wore only a silk shirt. They were expected to service the needs of the lowest levels of society, no matter what that need was. The cost was 25 cents to look, 50 cents to touch and $1.25 to have sex. "Sing song girls" was a term used to describe the crib girls who sang to advertise their services. Their life expectancy was 6 years once in the profession as a prostitute. Once they were no longer useful in the trade, the girl was placed in a small cell and given the choice of taking her own life or being murdered. (3,9)

Prostitution in Elko County, Nevada

Prostitution came to Elko County as early as the 1860's. One of the first houses to be established was Donna's Ranch. According to the owner (2) Donna's Ranch has been in continuous operation since 1867. The Ranch was originally established by the railroad to service the needs of the men constructing the railroad.

Donna's Ranch is located in Wells, Nevada. Wells was originally known as Humboldt Wells, after the nearby Humboldt River. It was used by the railroad as a watering station. It was a major transfer point for loading cattle onto the Central Pacific Railroad. Many of the cowboys would bring a herd of cattle to the railhead. Their pockets filled with money and their hearts filled with desire, they would most certainly visit Donna's Ranch. Many of the local ranches would establish a line of credit with the house by "donating" a few head of cattle. This had been a typical way of business for all the houses in Elko County up to the present-day. During the time of the Great Depression of the1930's, it was Donna's Ranch that made major donations of food and money that kept the town of Wells, Nevada from starving.

This house has enjoyed several local, as well as national, celebrities as patrons and owners. A local outrider for one of the major cattle ranches of the 1890's was a man known as "Diamondfield Jack". He was unjustly accused of the murder of two sheepherders. There were several occasions when it took a governor's intervention to prevent his hanging. As a result of the prolonged litigation a range war occurred between the Owners of the cattle ranches and the sheepherders. This war lasted for approximately ten years. Eventually, "Diamondfield Jack" was acquitted. A .44 caliber gun killed the shepherds. The gun carried by Diamondfield was a 45 caliber. Finally, two other cowboys admitted they had killed the shepherds. (2)

The world champion boxer Jack Dempsey was a previous owner of Donna's Ranch. In fact, today there is a special room in Donna's Ranch known as the Dempsey suite. He eventually received enough criticism about ownership of the house that he sold it (2)

Prostitution in Nevada is a legal issue left here to the discretion of the local townships and counties. (15) It is always been that way. For example in Clark County, which includes the city of Las Vegas, prostitution is illegal. In Washoe County, which includes the city of Reno, prostitution is also illegal. In Elko County, which includes the city of Elko, Bordello prostitution is legal.

In Elko the girls of the house cannot leave the house after 5:00 P.M. without notifying the local police. If notification is made, a girl may leave the house after 5:00 P.M. if she has an escort. Between the hours of 8:00 A.M. and 8:00 P.M. the girls may be out of the house without notifying the police.

Elko has four houses of prostitution. The majority of their business comes from tourists who come to Elko principally to gamble. There is some business done with truckers. However, the city of Elko has banned the use of CB radios for the purpose of solicitation for sex. Further, the city of Elko does not permit tractor-trailer vehicles to be parked on city streets. In contrast, the city of Wells, which is also located in Elko County, does permit the use of the CB radio for solicitation of sex. Further, two houses that are located in Wells are located north of the city adjacent to a state highway which has provided a designated turning lane for access to the houses. (17)

The majority of customers for these houses are over the road truck drivers. In fact, according to Mr. Geoff Arnold, the owner of Donna's Ranch, his house services approximately 6,000 truckers per month. (2)

In order to appreciate prostitution, as it really exists in Nevada, I decided to interview an owner of an active house of prostitution. I first made contact with Sergeant Dale Lotspeich, an employee of the Elko County Sheriff's Department. (15) It is Dale's duty to enforce the county regulations as they apply to the legalized system of bordello prostitution in Elko County. Dale informed me that in the thirteen years he has overseen the houses in Elko County he recalls only one case of assault in any of the houses. (15) Elko County, Nevada, covers an area of 16,000 square miles. That is an area larger than several Eastern U.S. states.

Sergeant Lotspeich has been involved in the enforcement of the law for several years. In the performance of his duties Dale has come to know all of the owners of the houses of prostitution in Elko County. Dale made it possible for me to have an interview with Mr. Geoff Arnold. Mr. Arnold owns houses in both Wells and Battle Mountain. Battle Mountain is a town of about 5,000 people. It is located 75 miles West of the city of Elko and is in Lander County. I chose to conduct my interview with Mr. Arnold at his house in Wells. Wells is a town about 50 miles East of Elko and is located in Elko County.

Upon arrival at Donna's Ranch the house the bartender greeted me. She invited me to have a drink at the bar. I declined. One of the girls came out to the bar area. She looked at me. I explained to her that I was there to interview Mr. Arnold for research purposes for this book. She smiled and went back down the hall to her room. Shortly after that, a trucker came into the house. He was not doing research for a book. He was given a drink by the bartender. She then asked if he wanted a "lineup".

Lineup is a term used to describe a process in which all of the available girls in the house come to the bar area and stand in line. The customer then inspects the girls and makes a choice of with whom he wants to "have a party". Have a party refers to the contract for sexual services. Once the selection is made, the girl and the customer go to her room where they come to terms for the particular service the client desires.

About this time Mr. Arnold arrived. He was quite pleasant. He first gave me a brief history of the house. He informed me that the house has been in continuous operation for over 150 years. He then took me back to some of the girl's rooms. Most were empty. The girls don't come on duty until 2:00 P.M. They usually work until 2:00 A.M. There are exceptions should a customer come through the door at 4:00 A.M. He showed me the showers. He explained that sometimes when a customer comes in he has been driving a truck for a long time. The girl he selects will escort him to the showers. He then showers. Once done with his shower, he is taken to the girl's room, where he undresses. She will do a visual inspection of the trucker. She is checking for any visible signs of disease or infection, especially in the genital area.

If he passes inspection, they then discuss the price for the services requested. The usual price is $150 for vaginal sex. Once in her room and a price is paid, the customer is shown some pornographic videos in order to sexually arouse him. Once aroused, the girl will place a condom on the customer and vaginal intercourse begins. The time to ejaculation is usually short. Once ejaculation is finished, the condom is removed and disposed in a sanitary container. The customer then dresses and leaves.

The girl takes the money to a special mailbox, which has slots for the girls to deposit the money by their name. She then marks on the board that she is available for the next customer. The average time allowed for a party is twenty minutes from start to finish. The girl keeps half the money and the other half goes to the house. The girls' income is reported on Form 1099 for tax purposes. Most girls are in the 40% tax bracket. The average income of the girls ranges into six figures. On average, a girl can make around $1,000 a day.

Mr. Arnold then took me to the kitchen. The kitchen was bright yellow with green trim. There was a large table covered by a bright red and white-checkered plastic tablecloth. There was a large pantry and several freezers. The girls apparently eat very well. They take turns cooking.

The overall impression of the room was that it would be more comfortable on the set of "Ozzie and Harriet" rather than in a brothel in the Nevada desert.

On one wall was a large array of coffee mugs hanging from pegs. The coffee mugs belonged to the "regular" customer. The collection represented most of the major national trucking companies and many of the minor ones. It was somehow comforting and "homey" for the truckers to know that they wouldn't have to share a coffee mug with anyone else, even if they would undoubtedly be sharing the vaginal areas of their favorite companion.

The kitchen had another amenity besides "personalized" coffee. That was the "eternal pot of chili." On the back burner of one of the stoves sat a rather large kettle containing the secret recipe chili. This kettle was always simmering and available…much like the girls of the house. Whatever the season, a trucker could always come to the house and expect a hot cup of coffee, an even hotter bowl of chili and, of course, the "hottest" sex. At least two of these three were free. The third was subject to negotiation.

On my tour I was offered all three. I chose the coffee. Somehow it seemed the best choice, especially since I didn't know how long the chili had been simmering and since I did know how long the other choice had been "simmering."

The kitchen offered one other curious feature. On a shelf near the impressive coffee mug collection, was a small 3" x 5" green tin file box. I asked its purpose. My tour guide informed me that the box contained the personal information of all the "regular" customer of the house. Each card also had the numbers one through ten printed on it. Of course, I had to ask the purpose of the numbering. My guide said it was for the "buy ten, get one free program." He further explained that with the purchase of ten parties at the regular price, the eleventh party was free.

My mind, still straining to maintain a serious and understanding countenance on my face, immediately grasped the parallel to "similar" marketing ploys used to sell lattes, mochas and cappuccinos.

However, the parallel did not sustain very long as I became increasingly aware that I wasn't standing in my favorite coffee shop.

Mr. Arnold then showed me to the "party room." The walls were painted in varying shades of brown. The floor was tiled in a brown and white checkerboard pattern. In one corner stood a pole lamp. Hanging near the round bed was a lamp suspended by a brass-colored chain.

The bed itself was circular. It sat on a motorized pedestal that made one complete revolution per hour. The bed was quite large and was covered by a red velvet bedspread. On top of the bedspread were many multicolored, striped and flowered throw pillows. The overall effect was far from sensual. In fact, the bed more closely resembled a miniature circus tend than a temple to Eros. It stood in sharp gaudy contrast to the drab and poorly lit appearance of the rest of the room. It was as though an alien flying saucer from the planet Red Velvet hand mistakenly landed on the drab surface of Planet Beige.

On the wall opposite the bed was rather small wet bar which is stocked only upon the occasion of a "party" being booked for the room. Leaning on the wall not far from the wet bar were some coaster brake bicycles. I was told they were being temporarily stored there because of lack of space in the customary storage shed. My mind, however, could not but speculate that perhaps these bicycles were used in some sort of sensual enterprise. The thought of nude bicycling as a form of foreplay was intriguing and painful at the same time. I winced at the thought, even though my tour guide had stated a far less erotic reason for their purpose in the room.

In general, my impression of the party room could be described as an eclectic garage sale rather than a temple of sensual delights. The party room can be booked with three or four girls for a weekend for up to $10,000.00.

I did have an opportunity to visit with one of the girls. "Holly" related that she had been in the business for several years. She had lived in Philadelphia and several large cities. She stated that she really liked working in Nevada. She related that the house of Mr. Arnold was more like a home and that she and the other girls were more of a family than co-workers. As I left Mr. Arnold invited me to come back for another visit. He invited me to bring my wife with me for another tour, since she had been previously invited and was unable to accompany me on this tour. (2)

3

Research

The popular opinion concerning prostitution in United States is negative. Based in part upon our Puritanical Ethics, and upon a long-standing history of illegal activity associated with prostitution, the average person in United States is opposed to prostitution. The state of Nevada however, has been much different in its opinion regarding prostitution. In fact, there has been a long-standing history of prostitution in Nevada since the 1850's.

The purpose of this dissertation is to examine the application of bordello prostitution as it is practiced in Nevada to the United States. In order to gain a better understanding of why bordello prostitution works in Nevada, it is necessary to examine the opinion of the citizens of Nevada regarding prostitution in general. To assess the popular opinion regarding prostitution by the citizens of Nevada, the <u>Reno Star-Gazette</u> conducted a survey. (22) The results of this survey were published in the newspaper on Sept. 16, 2002.

The results were as follows:
Fifty two percent of Nevadans are opposed to outlawing the state's legal brothels, according to a recent poll of 600 people interviewed for the statewide poll sponsored by the <u>Reno-Gazette-Journal</u> and News 4 (a local television station) by Research 2000 of Rockville, Maryland.

The margin of error is plus or minus four percent. Fifty-five percent of the men polled said they would oppose outlawing the brothels, and Forty-nine percent of the women polled said they felt the same as the men. Those with no opinion were eleven percent of the women and ten percent of the men.

I conducted a survey of Elko County residents regarding prostitution in Elko County. (Appendix 2) The survey was conducted in May of 2002 to assess the attitude of the general public toward prostitution in Elko County, Nevada. The surveys were distributed in connection with a Health Fair held at the local Wal-Mart store. In addition, surveys were also distributed at a local physician's clinic and at two local outpatient mental health clinics. A total of 100 surveys were distributed and returned. There were 80 female and 20 male respondents. The greatest percentage "39 percent" of the sample had some college education. About 74 percent of those surveyed came from homes where the parents were married throughout the respondents' childhood. About 86 percent of the survey was married and 13 percent were divorced. The highest percentage (68 percent) of the households had two or three children. Eighty percent of the respondents were residents of Elko County.

The religious preference of this survey included:

- Catholic: 34 percent
- Protestants: 26 percent
- The Church of Jesus Christ of Latter Day Saints: 12 percent
- Baptist: 4 percent
- Jewish: 2 percent
- "Other": 6 percent
- No preference: 16 percent.

The survey was broken down into the following age categories:

- Ages 21–30: 12 percent
- Ages 31–40: 26 percent
- Ages 41 and older: 58 percent.

The annual income levels in dollars were:

- 0 to 10,000: 8 percent
- 10,001 to 20,000: 12 percent
- 20,001 to 50,000: 22 percent
- 50,001 to 100,000: 48 percent
- 100,001 and above: 10 percent

The respondents were very much aware (ninety percent) that Nevada was the only state in United States where prostitution is legal. In fact, the legality of prostitution in Nevada is left by the state to the discretion of the local cities and counties. For example, the cities of Las Vegas and Reno are located in counties that prohibit prostitution. When asked if they were aware of any other places in the world where prostitution is legal most of the respondents (fourteen percent) knew of Amsterdam, Holland. This was followed by responses of Sweden at six percent of the survey, Europe at six percent, Germany, Holland, Mexico and Japan at four percent followed by Thailand, the Philippines and Denmark at two percent.

The survey asked people if they were aware of the number of brothels in Elko County.

- 42 percent replied 0–5
- 42 percent replied 6–10
- 16 percent replied 11 or more

The actual number of houses in Elko County is seven. (As of 2004 there are eight with the addition of another house in Carlin) There are two in Carlin, four in Elko and two in Wells.

The overwhelming percentage of those responding (ninety percent") had never been inside a brothel. However, this percentage must be tempered by the fact that women of the general public are not allowed access to the brothel. Therefore, eighty percent of those responding could not enter a brothel. Of the males surveyed, only eight percent had never been in a brothel, and thirty-seven percent of the males who had entered a brothel had had a sexual contact with a prostitute in a brothel.

One of the major issues addressed by the survey was whether or not prostitution should remain legal in Nevada. Results showed that *sixty-three percent* of those surveyed were in favor of keeping prostitution legal in Nevada. Remember, eighty percent of those surveyed were female and twenty percent were male.

On the issue of legalizing prostitution in United States, thirty-four percent were in favor and fifty-six percent were opposed. Regarding the issue of decriminalizing prostitution in United States, fifty-four percent were in favor and forty-six percent were opposed.

Sex workers in Germany, were prostitution has been legalized, are eligible for social security type benefits. My survey indicated only slightly higher approval than disapproval for a similar benefit for prostitutes in Nevada.

On the issue of whether or not a prostitute should have the right to sue their clients for nonpayment for services, sixty-four percent were in favor and thirty-six percent opposed. Regarding the right of prostitutes to unionize, the survey was equally divided in favor and against. This negative attitude may be reflected in the fact that Nevada is a right to work state and therefore there is a general negative attitude regarding unionization in the state.

The survey addresses the issue of taxation of brothels. The consensus (ninety-nine percent) was in favor of taxation of brothels. In fact, brothels are significant tax contributors to the federal government. Most of the sex workers in Nevada brothels provide 1099 tax forms and claim revenue as independent providers.

When asked if the respondents had *never* been in a brothel in Nevada, thirty-two percent said yes sixty-eight percent said no. Of the men responding twenty percent had had a sexual contact with a prostitute.

There appears to be a public perception that there is a link between the presence of prostitution in a community and the occurrence of violent crime. Forty-three percent held this concept whereas fifty-seven percent did not. Of those surveyed who saw a connection between the presence of prostitution in the community and the occurrence of violent crime i.e. murder, rape, assaults, robbery or illegal drug trafficking, sixty-three percent felt it decreased the presence of violent crime and only thirty-seven percent felt that prostitution in the community increased the incidence of violent crime.

An interview I conducted with an employee of the local sheriff's department (15) indicated indeed that the presence of legalized prostitution in a community did lower the incidence of violent crime. In fact according to Dale Lotspeich (15), a sergeant in the Elko County Sheriff's department, in the past thirteen years he can recall only one incidence of violent crime that occurred at a local brothel.

Another common opinion is that there is a connection between prostitution and organized crime. In my survey fifty-seven percent felt was no connection between organized crime and brothel prostitution in Elko County. Forth-three percent felt there was such a connection. According to the interview (15) there is no connection between the presence of prostitution and organized crime in Elko County.

Interestingly, despite apparent approval of brothel prostitution in our community, the respondents overwhelmingly (eighty-seven percent") were opposed to knowingly allowing a brothel located in their neighborhood. This supports the idea of brothel prostitution being placed in a designated "red light" district.

The most intriguing question on the survey was determining the major reason why there is an apparent indifference to the presence of brothels in Elko County. Of the respondents, twelve percent felt it was due to the lack of awareness on the part of the community. Twelve percent felt it was due to a lack of involvement in prostitution. Thirty-seven percent felt it was a live and let live attitude. Twenty percent didn't care. Five percent had a sense of futility to try and effect some change. Four percent felt it was due to the low profile kept by the brothel owners. Five percent felt it was preferable to having the prostitutes on the streets. Five percent felt it kept the rate for sexual crime, such as rape, down.

My survey showed that in Nevada the attitude toward legalized bordello prostitution is positive. Some might argue that prostitution is detrimental to marriage. However, my survey was comprised of eighty-six percent married respondents who responded favorably. Of the respondents, seventy four percent had come from a home where the parents had been married throughout the respondents' childhood.

Some might argue that prostitution is offensive to women. However, of the respondents, there were four times the numbers of women as compared to the men. Therefore, females were favorable to prostitution. Some may argue that prostitution is detrimental to families. However, sixty-eight percent of my respondents had two to three children at home.

Some may argue against prostitution on religious and/or moral grounds. However, my survey was comprised of thirty-four percent Catholics, twenty-six percent Protestants and twelve percent Church of Jesus Christ of Latter Day Saints (L.D.S.). That totals seventy-two percent, or nearly three quarters, of the respondents were members of strong traditional churches. Some may argue that a positive relationship with prostitution is more likely to be correlated with low income or that the higher the socio-economic status, the more likely there would be a negative attitude toward prostitution. However, my survey indicated that fifty-eight percent of the respondents had annual incomes above $50,000. Educationally nearly forty percent of the respondents had some college experience.

One might argue that maturity might be a factor or that a positive attitude toward prostitution would be more likely to be found among a younger age group. My survey indicated a twelve percent favorable response in the age group of 21–30 years of age but a fifty-eight percent favorable response among the age group of forty-one years and older.

I found it quite interesting that there was such a favorable attitude toward prostitution despite the fact that in my survey ninety percent had never been inside a brothel, either by choice or by being restricted from entry. Women are not allowed inside a brothel unless they work at the house. One might assume that without firsthand knowledge that a person would rely on the societal stereotypical opinions toward prostitution.

It was also significant to note that sixty-three percent of those surveyed were in favor of keeping legalized prostitution despite the fact that in the past five years there has been a large influx of population into Nevada from areas of the country that have traditionally been opposed to prostitution (22). Strangely fifty-six percent of those I surveyed were opposed to legalizing prostitution as a whole in the United States. It would appear that the only form of legalized prostitution that the people of Nevada favor is the type found in Nevada, i.e. legalized bordello prostitution. In fact, my survey indicated a fifty-four percent favorable attitude toward decriminalizing prostitution in the United States.

What is the difference between legalization and decriminalization? Essentially, to legalize prostitution would allow prostitution in all forms to exist without any restrictions in the United States. This would open the door to all forms of exploitation. On the other hand, to decriminalize prostitution would allow for the specification of what type of prostitution activities would carry legal sanctions and which would not. Thereby it would give the legal bodies in this country the ability to clearly specify that only bordello prostitution would be void of any criminal culpability. This would further enable the legal bodies the ability to restrict the forms of prostitution activities that are exploitive in nature. This would eliminate the exploitive forms of prostitution as well as be consistent with the favorable attitude found in my survey toward bordello prostitution as exemplified in the Nevada Model.

The question remains: *why this favorable attitude toward bordello prostitution in Nevada?* My survey indicated that a majority of the respondents (eighty-one percent) were unaware, uninvolved, didn't care or were just plainly indifferent to the presence of prostitution in their community. Of the remainder of the respondents, only five percent felt frustration about the presence of prostitution in their community. Clearly, then, ninety-five percent of those surveyed, had a favorable attitude toward the presence of prostitution in their community.

Perhaps one need only look at the historical presence of bordello prostitution in Nevada as a form of test case. Perhaps the one hundred fifty plus years that it has been in successful operation in Nevada has demonstrated the positive effect it can have in a community. Perhaps it has been acculturated into the very fabric of the community as much as any other forms of societal institution. If affected in the framework of the Nevada Model, bordello prostitution can be an effective means of deterrence to the deleterious impact of unrestricted prostitution as well as have a very favorable impact on the local communities. Obviously it works here in Nevada and can just as easily work elsewhere. The objective opinion of the population of Nevada indicates support of the idea of legalized bordello prostitution.

In order to get a more personal look at this Issue, I interviewed "Holly", one of the sex workers employed at "Donna's Ranch. (Appendix 3) My interview with Holly was quite interesting. It was the first time I had ever been in a brothel. I had a number of preconceptions that needed to be either confirmed or refuted. I had always thought that a "cat house" would be dark and dingy. However, the house where Holly worked was more motel-like than home-like. The appearance of the facility seemed more of an eclectic effort to form some cohesive presentation of either style or class. Unfortunately, it more resembled a garage sale waiting to happen. This may be an unfair characterization since this was, in fact, my first encounter of the bordello kind. I had to keep in mind that the primary function of the facility was not like that of an Ethan Allen Showroom. In the context of form following function, the house succeeded remarkably well. I am not faulting the intent or the effort. The results were at least functional in their effect.

As I entered into the facility the aroma of a wide variety of alcoholic beverages struck me. An even stronger was obtained through the combination of several divergent brands of perfumes, each competing for the position of dominant fragrance. Of course, intertwined with these fragrances was the presence of active and formerly active cigars, cigarettes and other forms of tobacco products.

As I approached the bar, I was struck by the "aging" of the facility. This facility had stood at this location since it was originally constructed by the Central Pacific Railroad to service the needs of its construction workers during the building of the transcontinental railroad. There was almost a museum-like reality to the place.

I received a warm greeting from the bartender who I am sure mistook me for a potential customer. She offered me a drink. I declined. She offered me a "line up". A "line up" is the process in which all of the available girls of the house present themselves for inspection and selection for services by the customer. I declined. I reiterated several times that my presence in the establishment was purely academic in nature. I knew I didn't really need to place such a strong emphasis on my purpose, but subconsciously it seemed to reassure me of the efficacy of my marriage in some specific areas I thought must be blatantly obvious to the bartender. I therefore had absolutely no reason to partake in the services being offered by the establishment through the "line up". I stated that I was there for an interview with "Holly", one of the sex workers at the house. The bartender nodded and briefly disappeared down an adjacent hallway.

In a few moments "Holly" appeared, dressed only in a bright red housecoat, and greeted me. I introduced myself. She then invited me to follow her back to a lounge area deep inside the facility. Along the way we passed a number of nameless doors that I assumed were the locations for services. Upon arrival at the lounge area Holly excused herself to retire to her room to put on something more comfortable. My mind instantly pondered what form of dress could be more comfortable than the attire Holly was already wearing?

Momentarily Holly reappeared in the lounge wearing a pair of pants and a sweatshirt. My mind was at ease. Holly had taken into account the uneasiness of my first experience in a bordello and had adorned herself in far less revealing attire. This became even more apparent as I looked about the facility and saw a number of Holly's coworkers arrayed in various combinations of lingerie obviously designed for other purposes than an academic interview.

A great sense of relief came over me as Holly suggested we retire to the backyard patio for some privacy during the interview. Along the way Holly pointed out some of the more interesting features of the house, including the "party room". The "party room" contains a very large circular bed as well as a private Jacuzzi tub. For an agreed upon fee, a party could be booked with several girls for an entire weekend. The usual costs for such a party ranges up to ten thousand dollars payable in advance.

We arrived at the patio and sat down on some very nice patio furniture. A privacy fence surrounded the area. The fence did little to obstruct the view of the truckers circling the facility to find an appropriate parking spot. Holly had also neglected to inform me that the house had been constructed immediately adjacent to the main line of the Union Pacific Railroad. This became very apparent when during the course of taping the interview the 9:00 P.M. freight train blew its whistle just as it approached the patio. The rumble and roar was, thank goodness, only transitory.

I explained that I would be recording the interview. Holly was very cooperative. I started the interview with an attempt to determine how Holly would portray the process of prostitution. She stated that it was "one of the ultimate expressions of love". (Appendix 3) She further made it clear that prostitution was non-discriminatory, that it was "for anybody, gays, blacks, everyone" (Appendix 3).

Holly is an attractive 26-year-old Caucasian female and a native of New England. Conservative, but supportive, parents raised her. She had some higher education and, at the time of the interview, was pursuing further education. Holly had previously had a career as a stripper. She became a sex worker because of the income potential and her "love of sex"(Appendix 3). She was single and had a male partner in San Francisco, California. Holly declined to respond to my question as to whether or not she had any children. I somehow felt that the subject of children was a sensitive issue and that either she had children whom she did not want to be connected to her present occupation or she had engaged in some emotional activities associated with children, i.e. abortion, adoption, etc. In any event, I respected her refusal to respond in that area of her life and did not pursue that area any further.

I was curious about a history of verbal, physical or sexual abuse, which may have led to Holly's career as a sex worker. According to Holly she had no history of any form of abuse. In fact, one could characterize her upbringing as being the stereotypical "All American Family" type.

I asked Holly about the interview process that someone might experience in order to obtain employment in the sex industry. Essentially, a girl calls a house and speaks to the madam or house owner. Once the basics are covered, the house owner will determine if a girl has any significant legal history. The owner will then request some photos of the girl to be sent via fax or E-mail. If the girl's appearance seems adequate, then she is invited to become a resident of the house. This is, of course, dependent on available room at the house. The girl must also pass a physical exam for the presence of any sexually transmitted diseases or H.I.V., as well as her general state of health.

Holly then described the variety of the girls working in the house. This enables the customer to "find whatever you want". (Appendix3)

I asked Holly how long she had been in Nevada. She stated she had been in Nevada for three years, mainly because it was legal here. She was quite adamant that she had no legal arrest record and that it was very important to her to be able to pass any background check that any potential employer might run on her.

Holly liked the remoteness of the Nevada brothels. This helped in ensure her anonymity. I'm quite certain that "Holly" is a pseudonym for a young New England woman who does not want her "All-American" family to know of her profession as a sex-worker. Holly related that in spite of the fact that she is a sex worker because she "loves sex" (Appendix 3) there are the usual occupational stressors of any type of job and hence the need for an occasional outlet. To that end, Holly takes one day off per week to go somewhere to do some alcoholic drinking, gambling and smoking. Holly makes it a rule to never consume alcohol while "on duty".

When I asked her as to the length of an average workday, she responded with the question of how I defined "work". If I meant the time she was "on duty", technically that is twenty-four hours a day. If 'work" is defined as the actual performance of sexual acts for pay, then the hours are highly variable. According to Holly, the average time spent with clients range from forty-five minutes up to two hours and forty-five minutes per day. That translates to a range of three to eleven customers per day at fifteen minutes per customer. That's correct! The average workday for a sex worker ranges from forty-five minutes to two hours and forty-five minutes per day!

Holly has been a sex worker for eight years, which means that she started in the business at age eighteen. Remember that before Holly went into the business as a sex worker, she had had a career as a stripper. She commented that she would never have gotten into the business if she did not have the support system behind her to help her find her true environment. The environment she wanted was one of instant gratification.

We discussed the type of services requested by customers. Holly stated that the preferences go in cycles. She stated that at the time of the interview about seventy percent of business was straight genital sex, twenty percent was oral sex, and fifteen percent was fetishes and eroticism. Holly stated she had only a couple of requests for anal sex and that any form of sex is really not a problem for her. The girls can be selective, even if chosen in a "line up". They can essentially refuse services by doing what is known as a "price walk". A "price walk" essentially means that a sex worker will take a customer back to her room and require a price for services that she knows the customer can't or won't pay. The result is that no services are performed.

Another reason why no services are performed is the physical genital inspection, commonly referred to as the "dick check". This activity consists of having the male place his penis in a small basin filled with alcohol and soap. The basin is commonly referred to in the jargon of the business as a "peter pan". The sex worker will then bathe the customer's penis checking for any visible signs of any outbreak of sexually transmitted disease, HIV or any form of genital herpes that would prohibit physical contact on the part of the sex worker. Holly always informs her customers that if any type of problem of that nature occurs, she will not provide any services and usually keeps half of the price paid and refunds the rest to the customer. In some houses a full refund is made. Holly likes to refer to herself as a "sex therapist". She discussed her concerns that the majority of Americans do not know how to properly install or use a condom.

Our discussion then turned to the income made by the average, not particularly attractive sex worker in a rural Nevada brothel. Holly estimated that such a worker, if she did not have any "baggage", meaning any addictions or exploitive companions, would have an annual income of $155,000.00 to $162,000.00. Holly was in favor of legalized prostitution in the United States.

She saw little connection between prostitution and organized crime. Holly felt that the climate within the houses was designed to promote personal growth for each worker. She felt the potential was certainly there for the development for each sex worker as an independent businesswoman. She had seen a number of workers come into the house to get away from bad boyfriends, bad situations and rise up from poverty and promote their educations. On the issue of prostitution and the incidence of violent crime, Holly felt the presence of prostitution actually lowered the incidence of violent crime.

Holly admitted she had encountered a few sex workers who are active alcoholics and or drug abusers. She "counsels" them to save their money and not waste it on alcohol or drugs. Holly claimed to have been employed at one time in a drug and alcohol counselor in a treatment center in San Francisco.

When I asked Holly about the apparent indifference to the presence of bordello prostitution in a community she theorized the indifference was a function of the tradition of the West to live and let live. Another reason she speculated was the tremendous financial contribution made by the houses to the tax coffers of the various communities. A third reason was the familiarity of the communities with the girls. Specifically, the girls of the house are seen in town buying groceries, going to the park or gambling at the local casino. I pressed her to state that Nevada, in general, was pretty accepting. Holly disagreed. She felt that it was not so much that people were accepting, as it was that people prefer to mind their own business. I asked Holly if she felt the Nevada Model of prostitution, which is essentially rural in nature, would transfer to a large metropolitan area such as New York City. She felt there would be a positive reaction as long as the operation was handled professionally.

Our discussion then entered the area of state-owned, or state-operated houses. Holly felt that state-owned or state-operated houses could work. She felt the sex workers would obviously be the state or city workers who would bring in the most money fir the city, county, or state. The more Holly reflected on the aspect of state-owned houses, the more she began to reject the idea of state-owned houses. Her principal reason was that the individual sex worker is far too independent. She states her opposition to state ownership by saying, "Just get your hands out of my panties." (Appendix 3) Holly felt there should be an increase in the number of houses, especially houses operated by women who have the experience in house operations.

Our discussion then turned to "street walkers", women and or men who solicit people on the street allowing the individual streetwalker to provide a variety of sexual acts to the customer for a fee. The "street walkers" are the lowest form of prostitute, and are the target of the greatest amount of exploitation and abuse. Holly had never been a "streetwalker". She was not opposed to them, but did feel they were the targets for violence due to their presence on the street without adequate protection. Her major objection to street prostitution was the lack of adequate protection for the workers, as well as the customer, through the lack of or improper use of condoms. Holly estimated that at least half of the "street walkers" would contract some form of venereal disease,

Holly felt that if a large enough number of legal houses was established across the country that the "street walker" would disappear. The girls would come off the streets and into a house where they could have a place to sleep, food, and protection. They could also get educations and establish alternative careers.

The issue of unionization of sex workers was discussed. Holly felt that in order for that to happen in the United States, that the sex workers need to hire a lobbyist. She felt it would be difficult to get the sex workers to contribute financially to support a lobbyist. She also felt it would be difficult to organize the workers into cohesive political constituencies.

The issue of non-payment for services did not appear to concern Holly. She stated that she would simply call the wives of her customers and would have no trouble getting the wives to pay for the services rendered to the husbands.

I asked Holly again why she became a sex worker. She attributed some of the reason to the fact that her parents had encouraged her to read. In so doing, she had encountered the stories of women in the West who were sex workers, later madams, who became very rich, powerful and famous. They were, in essence, Holly's role models. When I asked Holly about any treatment for mental disorders, she denied any. Specifically I suggested the mental disorder "nymphoma-nia". Holly objected to the entire notion of nymphomania as a causative factor for a woman to pursue a career as a sex worker. She asserted that sex is a natural choice made by women who know their sexual identity. Holly conceded that there are certain women in prostitution who have mental issues and are on some form of medication.

Holly's ambition is to someday operate her own legalized house of prostitu-tion in the Northeastern United States. I asked her how much longer she felt she would be in the business as a sex worker. She replied "three years". By the end of that time she feels she will have acquired enough information to successfully operate her own house close to her old hometown. She stated she would be hap-pier if she could operate her own legalized house of prostitution so that she could have her own home close by to live in.

Finally, I asked Holly what she would change about the industry. She responded that the collective thought of all the women in the industry is to fight for their civil rights and to fight for more awareness of and use of condoms. She felt that through increased individual income could come social power to lead to social change. She felt that women should have a bigger voice in the operation of the sex industry and eventually the country itself.

I asked Holly to comment on her own political aspirations. Her response was quick and decisive, "no!" She stated, "Who me? I don't want to get shot!" (Appendix 3) Apparently, Holly must have presidential aspirations.

I believe Holly was probably an exception to the general rule for sex workers. She was quite articulate on a number of issues. She was strongly opinionated and outspoken. I was fortunate to have been able to interview her first. I found it ironic that Mr. Arnold, the owner of the house in which Holly was working, had pointed me toward Holly as a good candidate to interview. His comment to me regarding Holly was that he felt she conceptualized herself as being a "super 'ho". (super whore) (1). I did not understand his reference until I had the opportunity to interview her and to encounter firsthand her strength of character and intelli-gence. Apparently, in the sex industry, the preferred qualities for a sex worker do not center on her intelligence or her ability to expound upon some social-psycho-logical theme as it manifests itself within the microcosm of a "cat house".

I found Holly to be an ambitious young woman who was highly goal-directed and self-motivated to acquire a position of power as a woman within a tradition-ally male-dominated industry. Holly represented the life of a sex worker in a large (eight to ten workers) house. I felt it was important to get a perspective on the life of a sex worker in a small house. I contacted "Paula". Paula and her son, "Larry" own and operate Sharon's. Sharon's is a small house with one to three workers located in Carlin, Nevada.

It was a cold and blustery winter night when my wife and I visited the house in Carlin. My glasses had broken earlier that day and I needed a chauffer. My wife graciously volunteered to drive, especially since her curiosity about the inte-rior appearance of a "house" was overpowering the possibility of spending the evening in an idling car with the heater straining to maintain a bearable tempera-ture against the winter chill. This was a definite possibility since no women, other than sex workers, are customarily allowed admittance to a "house". It is bad for business. Fortunately the owner had consented to her admittance. I believe this permission was due in part to the fact that there was not a customer in sight of the place. No customers meant that the "rule" could be bent a little.

Fortunately for us the exterior of the house was adorned with several strands of brightly colored Christmas lights. If it had not been for the extra holiday illumi-nations we would have possibly driven past the rather innocuous modular house due to the blowing snow and the fact that we had only a vague idea of the loca-tion of the house. The cashier at the local truck stop had even given us directions to the house.

"Paula", an older woman wearing something resembling a housecoat greeted us at the door. She was holding a glass containing clear intoxicating liquid. As we entered the room I was struck by the enormity of the bar inside the front door in contrast to the rest of the room. There was scarcely enough room to get past the bar to gain access to the rest of the rooms.

Paula represents the perspective of the house owner. She is not a madam. A madam must have first operated as a sex worker, which Paula has not. Paula and her son, Larry, named the house after Larry's late wife, Sharon. Sharon's is a small house with usually only one to three workers. Interestingly, all of the workers were black. Paula was more concerned about establishing a home-like environment for her establishment. She emphasized the humanitarianism and community-based charitable activities of she and especially her son.

Paula graciously offered by wife and I a drink. I accepted a cup of coffee and my wife declined. We never left he bar stools. No tour of the facilities was offered. However, through the course of the interview I did have several cups of coffee. Interestingly, with each cup of coffee I had, the owner had another glass of her clear liquid. As the evening progressed, the interview became less and less coherent, not as a result of my consumption of coffee.

The interview was punctuated by the appearance of two black workers at the house. I was particularly struck by the brightly colored negligees they wore, which stood in bold contrast to their dark complexions. Both were reluctant to make any comments, despite the urging of the owner to join in the interview. One of the workers named "Glitter" had been working at Samantha's off and on for a period of nine years. She goes home for Christmas and on vacations. Glitter stated that she had not worked the streets. She stated that Sharon's was a 24-hour house. That meant that at anytime day or night a customer could have their needs met. I asked Glitter why she had become a sex worker. She stated it was to earn money to go to school and her "love of sex". The subject of the type of sexual services that were being contracted for at the house came up. Glitter replied that I would find it incredible but that a large number of her customers don't want sex. They prefer to have conversation and a massage.

The issue of taxation generated a strong response in Paula. She stated that they pay the highest taxes. I mentioned some of the particulars of operation at Donna's Ranch, the place where I had interviewed Holly. I asked Paula to compare and contrast those with their operation. Paula stated that they don't do "line ups". Her comment was that it was too sleazy. Instead they have a photo album that the customer looks through and makes a selection. The bartender then goes back to the room of the girl selected and informs her that she has a customer who would like to "book a party" with her.

Paula reported that the truckers are their main source of income.
She related that a lot of their business came from sub-contractors to the local gold mines and from drillers. Paula had owned the house for about 15 years. They opened in 1989. She stated that she had seen a lot of changes in the sex-industry over that time. Specifically, Paula felt as though prostitution in Nevada

was going to die. She cited several reasons which included: the State not allowing them to advertise their services, the fact that they were not getting enough younger girls into the industry and the fact that the more mature workers were dropping out. Thus, the industry would die off for lack of workers.

I asked Paula what would she say were the reasons why bordello prostitution should be maintained in the community. Paula replied that the presence of bordello prostitution in a community cuts down on the rates of rape and molestation. She also stated that it brings in a lot of income for the city that it otherwise would not get. Paula characterized her house as more of a friendly roadside stop. She stated that they advertise a shower, a good conversation, great turn-around parking, iced tea, lemonade or coffee, all given very graciously.

I asked Paula why she felt the community had not protested against their place of business. She related it was due to the local popularity of her son, Larry. Larry is a strong community supporter. Paula stated that the community wanted them to operate. She even went so far as to state that the local Mormon Church wanted them to operate. I asked why. Paula's response was that the Mormon Church felt that the operation of Paula's house of prostitution would help protect the Mormon girls from the influx of workers and support services for the local gold mines. She stated that the Mormons wanted the house to open to keep the "virtue" of their teenage girls intact.

I asked Paula what she thought was the reason why the rest of the United States was so opposed to bordello prostitution. Did she feel it was due to a lack of understanding on their part? I found her answer to be interesting and amusing. "They're stupid…they don't understand, and I don't want to tell them to go out and do it (legalize prostitution) because it would cut down on our business, but every state should have legal prostitution. Don't think that every state doesn't have it, because they do. Those girls go to a hotel, they stay inside, the guy knocks on the door, he's made the deal with somebody else, he gives the girl a chip or something, but the girl has no protection. They don't know if this guy's a nut or what. Here there's a bartender out front, and if there's any problem I tell them the truth. I will sit down with him, talk it over and two of us are going to the door, and guess who isn't leaving." (Appendix 4)

Just like the other houses, the girls at Sharon's are checked every week by the Health Department for general health and sexually transmitted diseases. They are checked once a month for H.I.V. In the fifteen years of operation, Samantha's has never had a sex worker lose their work card due to the occurrence of a sexually transmitted disease. In addition, Sharon's has a sign at the entrance that reads "Condoms Are Mandatory." (Appendix 4).

Paula related that the girls check the customers for any visible sign of a communicable disease. There has been only one case in the fifteen years that was asked to leave for that reason. Paula's description of the process is rather amusing. They have a "peter pan" in which they put a little alcohol and some green soap, and if he has a cut or something, and when they yell "wee", we know it right away. (Appendix 4)

There is an organization of the owners of the brothels in Nevada called the Nevada Brothel Owner's Association. Its purpose is to promote legislation and other factors for the mutual benefit of all its members. Unfortunately, according to Paula it does not appear to be meeting the needs of all of its members. To quote Paula, "It hasn't done shit for us."(Appendix 4)

It became clear at this point that Paula was exhausted from our interview. After my fifth or sixth cup of coffee I concluded that the necessity to relieve the pressure in my bladder far outweighed an additional insights I might gain from the owner. Kathryn and I made our excuses and left Sharon's. We had been there for about two and a half hours and during that time not a single customer had come in for services. After an expeditious stop at the truck stop my chauffer and I braved the storm and returned to the sanctuary of our home in Elko.

I was interested to see if there would be any differences between responses obtained from a house operated in the heart of the city verses the more remotely located houses I had used in previous interviews. I also was curious to see if a house run by a house manager verses a madam would yield different results. A madam must have had some experience as a sex worker. A house manager does not have that experience. I felt that the manager might bring a more unbiased viewpoint to the issue. To that end I conducted an interview with "Samantha" at Sue's Fantasy Club in Elko.

My visit to Sue's Fantasy Club in Elko was a sharp contrast to the Carlin trip. First, I was by myself. My glasses were repaired and my wife's curiosity about bordello interiors had been satisfied. I went into the house and noticed a few people standing at the bar. They were far more occupied with each other than they were with the innocuous person standing in their midst requesting an audience with the house manager.

After a few moments the house manager greeted me and we immediately moved to a more secluded room. I was told that the room was the "parlor". The parlor is a meeting room for customers who wish to utilize the party room. The party room is located at the top of a flight of steps and emptied into the parlor. I explained that I had a cassette tape player and asked permission record her responses. She consented, but curiously did not turn down the volume on the television, which she watched throughout our interview. It was playing so loudly that I could barely hear her responses, despite the fact that she was sitting about two feet away from me.

She offered me something to drink. I declined, due in part to my previous experience with bordello coffee at the house in Carlin. I rationalized their poor quality of coffee with the idea that their principle product did not normally involve coffee beans. That is not to say, however, that the possibility did not exist.

The interview proceeded rather uneventfully with one striking exception. As I was straining to hear the manager's responses, out of the corner of my eye, I detected some movement near the staircase from the party room. I naturally turned and saw one of the workers coming down the steps. She was wearing a turquoise colored sheer pair of harem pants and a long-sleeved top. That was intriguing by itself, but the piece de resistance was the gray ten-gallon cowboy hat she was wearing. As she walked by she smiled and excused her self for interrupting our interview. I didn't mind.

Samantha has been the Operations Manager for Sue's Fantasy Club in Elko, Nevada for six months prior to our interview held on December 18, 2003. Sue's has been in operation for more than seventy years in downtown Elko, Nevada. The house averages between three to five girls in residence at any one time. In comparison, the large houses such as those in the vicinity of Reno or Las Vegas can have anywhere from fifteen to forty sex workers in residence at any one time.

I asked Samantha if she felt the Nevada Model of prostitution would work in other states. Samantha stated that she felt it would work great. She contrasted the per capita crime rate in Elko versus the per capita crime rate in Salt Lake City, Utah. In Elko, where prostitution is legal, the per capita crime rate is quite low compared to the high per capita crime rate in Salt Lake City, Utah where prostitution is illegal. Samantha's comment was quite strong, "If they are willing to pay for it, if its legal, if the girls are clean, then they are not out on the streets going after innocent people." (Appendix 5)

Samantha commented that it was hard to keep a place in operation since the law prohibits a house from advertising sexual services in the telephone book or other media. Instead they must advertise as a massage parlor or gentlemen's club.

Samantha discussed the large sums of money paid by the house to the various governmental bodies in the form of taxes. She stated that Sue's pays $2,500 a year for their brothel license. In addition they pay for a bar license, a liquor license, a normal business license, a spa permit and a health permit. In addition, they pay sales tax on all the liquor they sell and any merchandise like cigarettes, T-shirts and any souvenirs. (Appendix 5) Sue's does a lot of advertising on their Internet website. This is the only area of advertising that the State of Nevada has not been able to regulate.

We discussed how many customers they have per month. Samantha stated that it varies widely, but averaged almost 200 per month. Like the other houses, the price is negotiated by each girl with each customer depending upon the type of "party" he wants to "book". The average time allowed for each customer is around fifteen minutes. Samantha stated, "The average guy can get a straight lay in ten minutes for a hundred dollars." (Appendix 5)

Sue's Fantasy Club does provide a "lineup" for a gentleman who may have not been in a brothel before. The price is negotiated in the girl's room. Once a service is requested and a price agreed upon, payment is made. The girl takes the payment to the bartender who logs how much the party is for and how many minutes she is giving him.

The girls pay room and board every day. That cost is automatically subtracted from the total amount of revenue generated by the close of the books at the end of the day. Sue's opens a 3:00 P.M. and closes a 3:00 A.M. and is therefore not a 24-hour house. However, if the business is there, the house will remain open.

We discussed the incidence of gambling addiction and or alcoholism among the sex workers. Samantha felt that the percentage was high. She attributed the high rate of alcoholism to the fact that each customer that a sex worker has each day buys her a drink. She does not want to appear rude by refusing the drink. If you multiply one drink by up to ten clients a day, times seven days a week, that means the sex worker averages ten drinks a day, and seventy drinks in the average workweek.

Samantha stated that typically a girl would book four to five parties a day. That is due to the fact that the girls can get sore. The overall operation of Sue's was similar to the other houses in terms of dealing with unruly customers. It was also similar to the others in checking customers for possible health hazards. If there is a health hazard, the customer is asked to leave and given a full refund. Most of Sue's Fantasy Club business comes from businessmen and convention-eers. There are not many truck drivers since Sue's is in a residential area where over the road trucks are not allowed to park.

Samantha spent a great deal of time in our interview describing the wide variety of personalities that must be dealt with among the sex workers. Some have addictions issues while others are compulsive shoppers. One of the girls is saving up $3,000 for breast augmentation surgery. Samantha has tried to convince her that her customers don't care. They are not buying her time to admire the immensity of her breasts. But, the young lady remains determined to have the surgery. One interesting idiosyncrasy of the bordello is the "Queen." The "Queen" is the high booker for the house and enjoys a certain status among the other girls of the house.

I asked Samantha what she felt was the future for the houses. She stated that she felt the houses eventually would go away. She felt that the other states would never legalize prostitution. I asked why she felt that way. She replied, "Because of the morality of it. Unfortunately, especially like in the Bible Belt, like the south-ern states you know, they will never allow it to become legalized and I think even-tually because of the strip clubs and strip bars or whatever they want to call them, eventually they just kind of fade away." (Appendix 5) Samantha did not feel the State of Nevada would close the houses. Samantha commented, "They'll (the bordellos) just die out. The Internet has so much sexual material that the brothels have lost their importance in society." (Appendix 5)

According to Samantha, the brothel has become more of a tourist curiosity. Her final comment was that on the day the last brothel closes it would be like "a piece of history will have died. It's like the Mustang (Ranch). It's a part of history that's died."
   (Appendix 5)

The interview concluded and I got up to leave. As I walked to the bar area and the exit, the gray cowboy hat brushed past me on her return trip to the party room. I always have liked the color gray.

Samantha's comments echoed the thoughts of Paula at Sharon's House in Carlin, Nevada. I believe the Nevada Model of prostitution can survive if it becomes standardized and nationally adopted.

The future of prostitution in Nevada is bright. The house owners are moving in the direction of mega resorts. These resorts would be luxury hotels of a size comparable to the 4,000-plus rooms size of the hotels in Las Vegas, Nevada. These resorts would have all of the amenities including 5-star restaurants, high-end retail stores, PGA golf courses, top entertainment and family attractions.

Unlike the Vegas-style resorts, these resorts would include legalized prostitution available in your room. The costs could be charged to your room as a "massage". This would give a whole new meaning to the term "room service". This service, if done discreetly would function without disturbing the "moral" sensibilities of the other guests.

4

Conclusions

My study of prostitution in Nevada has revealed several interesting facts. Although most of the United States is opposed to legalized prostitution, Nevada remains in favor of continuing to allow brothel prostitution in rural areas of the state. This is especially interesting in light of the fact that fifty percent of Nevada's population of two and a half million has immigrated to the state from areas of the country that have been traditionally opposed to prostitution. This population influx has occurred since 1995. (22)

The implications for the rest of the country seem obvious. The high cost of criminal prosecution in the rest of the country far exceeds the cost of policing prostitution per capita in Nevada. The model of bordello prostitution in Nevada could be implemented in other places in the country by utilizing existing governmental agencies to:

- Lower the incidence of violent crimes against women
- Reduce the incidence of sexually transmitted disease and AIDS
- Improve the overall image of a community as a result of the lowered number of visible "streetwalkers"
- Increase tax-based revenues generated in communities that could then be used to support school, roads or other types of community services

The purpose of this book has been to explore the possibility of implementing the Nevada Model of Prostitution in the United States and possibly worldwide. During the course of my investigation several unspoken facts began to surface. One is the tremendous variability in the provision of what would rationally be assumed to be a standard procedure. Another was the variability in the atmosphere of the houses themselves, ranging from small home-like environments to large business establishments. The overwhelming feeling I had was a sense of pathos. There was a pervasive sense of sadness among the sex workers and some of the owners. They all made attempts to disguise this feeling by referring to their love of sex, or to the code of conduct which dictated that all they were concerned about was the money. Some even went so far as to characterize their houses as being "just like a home" to them. All of this points to the need for standardization in the industry.

I believe there could be a vast improvement in the general attitude of all sex workers if a uniform package of benefits as well as a universal set of operational procedure was adopted. Unfortunately, at least from the viewpoint of some of the owners, it appears that these essential functional adjustments seem impossible given the fiercely individualized and competitive nature of the industry as a whole, from the sex workers to the house owners themselves.

With the implementation of federal regulation on a national basis, I believe it would be possible to formulate national standards for the industry which would greatly enhance the general working conditions for the workers as well as generate a level of confidence in the minds of the consuming public as to the quality and safety of the product being delivered.

Make no mistake. This book is not arguing the morality of prostitution. That remains an individual decision. If one is to consider the morality of this institution, one must argue the merits of previous attempts to legislate the morality of human behavior in this country. A strong case in point was the institution of "prohibition" during the 1920's. This was a deliberate attempt to legislate the morality of the use of alcohol. The result was the creation of a huge influx of criminal activity, tremendous loss of life and tremendous financial costs for enforcement. People still drank alcohol, even though it was illegal and "immoral". In the end, the situation became untenable and "prohibition" was rescinded. So it is for prostitution.

Try as we might to legislate and enforce against it, there is a huge criminal involvement and tremendous cost of enforcement. People have used prostitutes since the dawn of time. They will continue to do so despite any and all attempts at "prohibition", from here on to be known as "*hohibition*", a term suggested by my son-in-law, Micah.

The logical alternative is to adopt a model of prostitution to meet a fundamental societal need and at the same time avoid the pitfalls of vain attempts to legislate morality. The Nevada Model of Prostitution works. It could just as effectively work in the rest of this country.

This is, of course, a "modest" proposal.

I believe I have taken a fair and objective approach to this issue. I consulted previous research and conducted my own original research. There is an historical precedence for the operation of prostitution in the United States. That same historical precedence has been as much a part of the heritage of the West as cowboys, Indians, miners and settlers. Perhaps there is some effect of history on the practice of modern day prostitution in the West. But the practical reality is that no industry survives in today's competitive market place if it cannot generate a desirable product in a safe and secure manner.

The Nevada Model of Prostitution generates thousands of dollars per year in income and in tax revenues. One need only do a simple extrapolation from the $160,000 per year income as stated by Holly in her interview. Consider that half of the income is automatically given to the house. The IRS takes an additional 40%. The State of Nevada is trying to take an additional 7%. That means that the average worker earns an income of $448,000 and $128,000 goes to the federal government each year. It also means that the brothel owner generates $64,000 to the federal government per worker per year. The latest estimate is that there are 1,000 legal brothel workers in the State of Nevada. (21). That brings the total of Federal revenue generated per year by the Nevada Model to $192 million. What other business operating in the United States with 1,000 employees and about fifteen managers generates that level of revenue? Nevada has an overall population of 2.5 million. The United States has a population about one hundred times larger. Using just the same ratio as it works here in Nevada, the estimated Federal revenue from legalized Bordello prostitution would be $19.2 billion per year.

The actual figure would be astronomical based on the high probability that larger populations would generate far more owners and workers. What type of federal programs could that level of financing fund?

This book represents an initial foray into an area of human experience that has carried both extremely negative as well as extremely positive connotations. I believe that the evidence, which I collected from my interviews and survey, has supported my initial hypothesis. The viability of bordello prostitution as a legitimate social institution has stood the test of time. The impact upon the incidence of violent crime, sexually transmitted diseases and the costs of law enforcement makes it a force to promote a positive social environment in the communities in which it operates. Even more significant is the tremendous income potential it generates in the form of fees and taxes. This income would reduce the property tax burden for the average taxpayer and, at the same time, fund a wide variety of current and potential governmental programs designed to alleviate a wide array of basic human needs.

This book is meant to stimulate dialogue among the various states to consider an approach to dealing with prostitution from a standpoint of prostitution not being a social anathema, but rather as a legitimate force for societal improvement.

There are several areas which merit further study. The most salient area would involve the development of a plan for the implementation of the Nevada Model for the rest of the country. This would involve a feasibility study to consider the best areas for location of the houses, as well as the development of standards of operation. The study would need to address the issue of community acceptance.

The presence of a house of prostitution in a "respectable" urban neighborhood would most certainly create a strong community reaction. The issue of the presence of a large number of vehicles on a quiet suburban street at all hours of the day and night could create quite a controversy. The basic construction of the house would have to be studied so that it would be consistent with the predominant architectural style of the adjacent neighborhood. Even something as simple as the signage on the home that would denote its purpose would have to be carefully considered.

In a more urban environment these types of considerations may not be necessary. Placement of a bordello within an urban office complex would certainly be less conspicuous than in a quite suburban neighborhood. The hours of operation of the bordello might need to be coordinated with the "usual" business hours of the surrounding tenants.

There could be a security concern on the part of the regular tenants if a 24-hour a day bordello was located next door to their business. As in the case of the suburban placement, careful consideration would have to be made in the area of the signage indicating the nature of services being provided by the bordello. The possibility exists that the other tenants could complain about the presence of the bordello hurting their respective business due to some sort of moral backlash or boycott of the entire building by some fundamentalist groups.

Another issue would be the recruitment process for sex workers. There would have to be a specialized employment agency created to screen the applicants in terms of physical health issues as well as any legal history that might eliminate the applicant. The creation of an administrative body to oversee the standards of operation of all the houses would also need to be considered. Within that consideration would be the coordination of the required ongoing medical services for the sex workers.

One of the major areas of study for the feasibility study would certainly focus on the fundamental issue of public versus private ownership. The issues that I have been previously discussing lend themselves to a publicly owned format. Under the public format there would be a number of other areas for investigation.

A time frame for the implementation of these services would need to be establishes. Another area of concern would be the designation of the appropriate law enforcement agency to oversee the operation of the business. There would also need to be a study of the type and scope of advertising that would be necessary to alert the general public to the plan of implementation for the services.

One of the major initial hurdles that need to be addressed would be a plan to lobby the respective state legislatures in order to provide the necessary legislation to create the legal format to allow for the creation of the houses within their legal jurisdictions. This would entail a great deal of public opinion surveys regarding bordello prostitution. An instrument similar in nature to mine would need to be generated. The question remains whether enough favorable public opinion could be generated to enable the lawmakers to feel confident in the creation of such a system based on the Nevada Model. I am sure that reference to my Nevada research would be beneficial to such an effort.

Another major area for research would be to survey the current pool of sex workers to determine if they would be willing to participate in such a national system. Another concern would be their reaction to national standards of operation. The dynamics involved in a form of unionization of the sex workers would also require study. The public implementation of the Nevada Model would be a very long process involving a great deal of public relations. There would also be some start-up costs involving the creation of a bureaucratic structure to administrate such a system, possibly called the "Sex Industry Administration Agency", or the S.I.A.A. My personal recommendation would be to focus on lobbying the state legislators in order to create a favorable climate for the legal adoption of the Nevada Model. The advantages are numerous.

Once the Nevada Model were nationally legalized, the way would be clear for the rapid development of the houses by the private sector. The start-up costs would fall upon the respective private developer. The legal enforcement control would fall automatically to the law enforcement agencies already established in place within the political jurisdictions where the houses would be in operation. The medical issues would be dealt with through private contracts between the respective houses and a local health care provider. In general, the private sector would essentially absorb the costs of the system and pass along a considerable amount of revenue to the federal and/or possibly the respective state governments through channels already been established, like the Internal Revenue Service.

All of these considerations fall within a macro system level of consideration. There are equally some very necessary areas for research on the micro level. One of the more obvious studies would involve a survey of all of the sex workers in Nevada to develop a psychological profile of the average sex worker. This profiling information could then be used within the selection process for the screening agency responsible for the hiring of sex workers on a national basis. This may seem to be a rather cold or indifferent approach, however, as my research indicated the composition of the staff of a bordello is composed of a wide variety of individuals. These variations can lead to a number of personality clashes within a house. These clashes can become a management nightmare. The efficiency in the delivery of the product would be greatly enhanced if houses could be structured along the lines of psychological compatibility.

A study should also be done on the owners of the houses. It would be interesting to obtain a psychological profile of the average owner of a bordello. This study would help to characterize the psychological make-up of the average person who owns the bordello.

One of the more interesting issues in such a study would be the reason why a person would consider making a living by being involved in the sex industry as an owner.

My study seemed to reveal a very powerful issue that seems to be disrupting the Nevada Sex Industry at this time. It involved the agency known as The Nevada Brothel Owners Association. I spoke to Mr. Geoff Arnold, the current President of the Nevada Brothel Owners Association. (1) My impression of the association was that it was an effective tool to lobby the Nevada Legislature to maintain a political climate favorable to the Sex Industry. However, in speaking to two other owners, or their immediate subordinate, I was struck by the degree of dissention and downright hostility that they held for the Association itself. These concerns need to be addressed and corrected, if possible, if the Nevada Model is to ever be led by an owners' association on a national level. Such an association, perhaps called "The United States Brothel Owners Association" (U.S.B.O.A.) would need to have a high degree of internal cohesiveness and unity in order to effectively lobby for legislation favorable to the Sex Industry on a national level.

Another very obvious study would be focused on the psychological makeup of the average individual who seeks the services of a prostitute. This study could concentrate on two very important issues. *One area of study* would be the reason why a person would choose a particular form of delivery to satisfy his/her sexual needs. Why does one man pick up a streetwalker, knowing full well that he stands a higher probability of contracting some form of sexually transmitted disease from them rather than if he were to frequent a bordello? Is that choice predicated upon the mere fact of availability, or is there something more psychosexually stimulating in procuring your sex in an inherently more dangerous sexual environment? The *second interesting area* would be to survey these customers to develop the psychological profile of the average person who is willing to pay to have his/her sexual needs met. There are a number of significant contexts in which such information would have great value in explaining the reasons why married individuals solicit sex from a prostitute. In many divorce cases one of the prime reasons involve sexual infidelity with a lover or a prostitute.

If a researcher could develop an instrument that could adequately profile the psychological makeup of an individual that would identify, within a certain confidence range, the more salient features of an individual who is likely to procure sexual services of a prostitute then one could make a probability projection of the likely occurrence of this behavior within the marital context for that individual, i.e. the "*I Scale*" or Infidelity Scale.

Within the context of the law enforcement community, if a psychosexual profile could be developed from this research that could adequately characterize the individual who has a high probability of procuring the services of a street walker, then that agency could develop a list of probable suspects in the event of some sort of violent crime perpetrated on a street walker in a particular case. This predictive potential may help to reduce the incidence of such types of crime, as well as decrease the time between the perpetration of such crimes and the conviction of such perpetrators.

A direct spin-off study of my research would be to study the reasons why there seems to be an inverse ratio between the presence of bordello prostitution within a community and the occurrence of violent crime. What is it about a certain type of individual that stimulates him to become physically combative with a woman? This woman in many cases is his spouse. The implications for the occurrence of domestic violence seem obvious. Bordello prostitution could be used as an effective tool to reduce the sexual frustration that may prompt a certain type of individual to commit violence against his sexual partner, or a sexual surrogate such as a streetwalker or rape victim.

If a study could be used to develop a psychosexual profile of such an individual, the rates of domestic violence as well as the incidence of violent street crime including assault and or rape would be dramatically reduced.

Another direct spin off of my research would involve the connection between the presence of bordello prostitution and the occurrence of H.IV. and AIDS. My study showed a very minimal occurrence of any form of sexually transmitted disease including H.I.V. and AIDS within the context of the bordello workers. In fact, rigorous precautionary measures are taken to ensure against the occurrence of any form of sexually transmitted disease. A study could be done involving the utilization rates by gay men and male bordello prostitutes. There are some intriguing dynamics that might arise. One of the most intriguing would be to promote homosexual contact between gay men and male bordello prostitutes. The implications would include a strong probability of reducing the incidence of H.I.V. and AIDS within the gay community. Until an effective cure can be developed, a viable preventive procedure seems a highly logical alternative. One of the obvious areas for study would be the apparent indifference by any organized religion to the presence of bordello prostitution within the community.

When I did my research, I was amazed that only five percent of those I surveyed (Appendix 2) had any sort of frustration associated with the presence of bordello prostitution in the community. Combine this with the fact that seventy-two percent of those surveyed identified themselves as members of mainstream fundamental churches (Appendix 2). One explanation that I found in my research (Appendix 4) was a belief (by one of the brothel owners) that the church, specifically the Church of Jesus Christ of Latter Day Saints promoted the presence of a brothel in the community as an indirect form of protection of their young female members from sexual assault. I find that interesting, but obviously this area needs further study. There is always the official position of the church and the practical application by its membership of that policy within the real world. It would appear that a lack of an official policy is a de facto policy. Is there a connection between religion and prostitution? I believe there is. Curiously, however, there appears to be an exception made by those I surveyed. (Appendix 2) The fundamental question seems to hinge upon an apparent logical contradiction. Does the lack of evil imply the presence of good?

How can any organization imply the presence of good and yet simultaneously apparently condone the presence of evil? If the anonymity and or low profile kept within the community by the houses of prostitution constitutes a lack of apparent evil, does that, in fact, allow the churches the luxury of implying the presence of good within the community? Is the lack of any apparent direct opposition to the presence of brothel prostitution within the community by the churches predicated upon the premise that the function of organized religion is to promote the good and, at the same time, accept the reality of the evil nature of man and his creations, such as bordello prostitution? If such is the case, then the only official policy that the churches can have is one of making the participation in brothel prostitution an individual moral choice for its membership. The implications of that policy should eliminate any official church position as a discrete entity within the community in regard to the presence or even the absence of brothel prostitution within the community.

Fundamentally, and ultimately, the participation by an individual of any religious affiliation in the activities of bordello prostitution is a matter of individual

moral choice. That does not mean the church does not attempt to discourage participation in the activities of the brothel by its membership. Many churches use guilt and/or the fear of eternal damnation as powerful tools of discouragement. I find it ironic that despite these control mechanisms there is still participation in brothel prostitution by the membership of these churches.
(Appendix 2).

The position that I took on the adoption of the Nevada Model of Prostitution for the rest of the country is entirely based upon the church's position that participation is strictly an individual moral choice. I did not argue for or against the morality of the presence or operation of brothel prostitution within the communities of rural Nevada. My paper advocates that the greater good of the community would be served by continuing to allow the operation of brothels within our communities. In fact, I have argued that the greater good of the country as a whole would be served by the adoption of the Nevada Model on a national basis. I agree with the churches that participation in brothel prostitution remains fundamentally a matter of individual moral choice. I agree further with the de facto reality, which is recognized by the churches of rural Nevada, that the existence of bordello prostitution is a part of the social climate within our communities.

Prostitution as a social institution has existed for centuries. This book has recognized that reality and has only extended the logic of its operation to the potential application of that institution to the amelioration of the human condition in this country and eventually the world. To oppose this reality would be as illogical as to deny the existence of gravity.

REFERENCES

1. Alexander, Priscilla, Prostitution: A Difficult Issue for Feminists, Frederique Delacoste and Priscilla Alexander,
    Sex Works, Writings by Women in the Sex Industry,
    Cleis Press, 1987, p. 188, 1967

2. Arnold, Geoffrey, Owner, Donna's Ranch of Wells and Battle Mountain, Nevada President, Nevada Brothel Owners Association, Interview with Daniel Tutty, September 16, 2002

3. Asbury, Herbert: The Barbary Coast, 1933

4. Bancroft, Caroline: Six Racy Madams of Colorado, 1965

5. Butler, Ann: Daughters of Joy, Sisters of Misery: The History of Prostitution in the American West 1865–1900, 1987

6. Butte Daily Miner: July 31, 1880

7. COYOTE survey of local prostitutes: San Francisco, 1995

8. Dobie, Charles: San Francisco's Chinatown, 1936

9. Hirate, Lucy Cheng: Free, Indentured, Enslaved: Chinese Prostitution in Nineteenth Century America, Signs 5, 1979

10. Holly: Sex Worker, Donna's Ranch, Wells, Nevada Interview with Daniel Tutty, September 19, 2002

11. "Interviews with local Prostitutes", Portland, Oregon, 1969

12. James Janella: Prostitutes and Prostitution, Deviants in a Hostile World, World Press, 1977

13. Knox, Noelle, "In Belgium, Brothels are Big Business", USA Today, November 5, 2003

14. Lambert, Bruce: "AIDS in Prostitutes, Not as Believed, Studies Find", <u>New York Times</u>, September 20, 1988

15. Lotspeich, Dale: Sergeant, Elko County Sheriff's Department, Interview with Daniel Tutty, September 6, 2002

16. Paula, Owner, Sharon's Bar and Brothel, Carlin, Nevada, Interview with Daniel Tutty, October 14, 2003

17. Mellon, Deborah: <u>The Legend of Molly b' Dam</u>, 1989

18. Morgan, Murray: <u>Skid Row: An Informal Portrait of Seattle</u>, 1951

19. Parkhill, Forbes: <u>The Wildest of the West</u>, 1951

20. Petrik, Paula: "Capitalists with Rooms: Prostitution in Helena, Montana, 1865–1900", <u>Montana Magazine</u> 1981

21. Relevant Nevada Revised Statues: "Pandering, Prostitution and Disorderly Houses", Pre-law Advising, 6/9/2003

22. Research 200: Survey of Attitudes Toward Prostitution in Nevada, a survey conducted for the <u>Reno Gazette-Journal</u> Newspaper and News Center 4 Television of Reno, Nevada Results reported in the newspaper September 16, 2002, Rockville, Maryland, 2003

23. Richardson, Albert: <u>Beyond the Mississippi</u>, Persia Books, 1869

24. Samantha: House Manager, Sue's Fantasy Club, Interview with Daniel Tutty, December 18, 2003

25. Seagraves, Anne: <u>Soiled Doves, Prostitution in the Early West</u>, 1994, WESANNE PURBLICATIONS, Hayden, Idaho

26. Seagraves, Anne: <u>Women of the Sierra</u>, 1990 WESANNE PUBLICA-TIONS, Hayden, Idaho

27. Snell, Joseph W.: <u>Painted Ladies of the Cowboy Frontier</u>, 1965

28. <u>Territorial Enterprise</u>: Virginia City, Nevada, June 7, 1877

29. The Centers for Disease Control and Prevention, HIV/AIDS Surveillance Report, 1993, (No. 3), pp. 7, 11, 17, 123

30. The San Francisco Chronicle: October 17, 1932 and December 5, 1869

31. Western History Departments, Denver Public Library and the Colorado Historical Society, Denver, Colorado:
    Denver Daily Times, September 4, 1886
    Rocky Mountain News, April 28, 1898 and July 7, 1876
    Denver Republic, May 4, 1889
    Denver Times, January 24, 1891

APPENDIX A

*Relevant Nevada Revised Statutes
(2003)*

CRIMES AGAINST A PERSON

200.310. Degrees. [Kidnapping]

PANDERING, PROSTITUTION, AND DISORDERLY HOUSES

201.295 Definitions 201.300 Pandering: Definitions, punishment; exceptions Sheriff v. Hilliard, 96 Nev. 345, 608 P2d 1111 (1980) Stanifer v. State 109 Nev. 304, 849 P2d 282 (1993) 201.310 Pandering: Placing spouse in brothel; penalties.201.320 Living from earnings of prostitute.201.340 Pandering: Furnishing transportation; penalties 201.354 Engaging in prostitution or solicitation for prostitution: Penalty, exception. Glegola v. State, 110 Nev. 344,871 P.2d 950 (1994) Stanifer v. State. 109 Nev. 304,849 P2d 282 (1993) 201.356 Test for exposure to human immunodeficiency virus required, payment of costs, notification of results of test.201.358 Engaging in prostitution or solicitation for prostitution after testing positive for exposure to the human immunodeficiency virus: Penalty, definition. Glegola v. State, 110 Nev.344, 871 P.2d 950 (1994) 201.430 Unlawful advertising of prostitution. Princess Sea Industries, Inc., v. State, 97 Nev.534, 635 P2d 281 (1981)

REGULATION AND LICENSING OF BUSINESSES AND OCCUPATIONS

244.345, Dancing halls escort services, entertainment by referral services and gambling games or devices; limitation on licensing of houses of prostitution. Princess Sea Industries Inc., v.State, 97 Nev. 534,635 P2d 281 (1981)

CRIMES AND PUNISHMENTS

193.130 Categories and punishments of felonies

CONDUCT OF TRIAL

175.301 Abortion or enticing person for prostitution: Testimony of person upon or with whom offense allegedly committed.

CRIMES AGAINST THE PERSON

NRS 200.310. Degrees. [Kidnapping]

1.) A person who willfully seizes, confines, inveigles, entices, decoys, abducts, conceals, kidnaps or carries away a person by any means whatsoever with the intent to hold or detain…and a person who leads, takes, entices, or carries away or detains any minor with the intent to keep, imprison, or confine him from his parents, guardians, or any other person having lawful custody of the minor, or with the intent to hold the minor to unlawful service, or perpetrate upon the person of the minor any unlawful act is guilty of kidnapping in the first degree, which is a category A felony.

2.) A person who willfully and without authority of law seizes, inveigles, takes, carries away or kidnaps another person with the intent to keep the person secretly imprisoned within the state, or for the purpose of conveying the person out of state without authority of law, or in any manner held to service or detained against his will, is guilty of kidnapping in the second degree which is a category B felony (LINK).

PANDERING, PROSTITUTION, AND DISORDERLY HOUSES

201.295. Definition.

As used in NRS 201.295 to 201.440, inclusive, unless the content otherwise requires:

1. "Adult" means a person 18 years of age or older.

2. "Child" means a person less than 18 years of age.

3. "Prostitute" means a male or female person who for a fee engages in sexual intercourse, oral-genital contact or any touching of the sexual organs or other intimate parts of a person for the purpose of arousing or gratifying the sexual desire of either person.

4. "Prostitution" means engaging in sexual conduct for a fee.

5. "Sexual conduct" means any of the acts enumerated in subsection 1.

201.300 Pandering: Definition, punishment, exception.

1.) A person who: (a) Induces, persuades, encourages, inveigles, entices or compels a person to become a prostitute or to continue to engage in prostitution;(b) By threats, violence, or by any device or scheme, causes, induces, persuades, encourages, takes, places, harbors, inveigles, or entices a person to become an inmate of a house of prostitution or assignation place, or any place where prostitution is practiced, encouraged or allowed; (c) By threats, violence, or by any device or scheme, by fraud or artifice, or by duress of person or goods, or by abuse of any position of confidence or authority, or having legal charge, takes, places, harbors, inveigles, entices, persuades, encourages or procures a person to enter any place within this state in which prostitution is practiced, encouraged or allowed for the purpose of prostitution; (f) Receives, gives or agrees to receive or give any money or thing of value for procuring or attempting to procure a person to become a prostitute or to come into this state or leave this state for the purpose of prostitution, is guilty of pandering:

2.) A person who is found guilty of pandering:(a) An adult:(1) If physical force or the immediate threat of physical force is used upon the adult, is guilty of a category C felony and shall be punished as provided in NRS 193.130.(2) If no physical force or immediate threat of physical force is used upon the adult, is guilty of a category D felony and shall be punished as provided in NRS 193.130.(b) A child: (1)if physical force or the immediate threat of physical force is used upon the child, is guilty of a category B felony and shall be punished by imprisonment in the prison for a minimum term of not less than 2 years and a maximum term of not more than 20 years, and may be further punished by a fine of not more than $20,000.(2) If no physical force or immediate threat of physical force is used upon the child, is guilty of a category B felony and shall be punished by imprisonment in the state prison for a minimum term of not less than 1 year and a maximum term of not more than 10 years and may be further punished by a fine of not more than $10,000.(3)This section does not apply to the customer of a prostitute.201.310

Pandering: Placing spouse in a brothel: penalties

1. A person who by force, fraud, intimidation, or threats, places, or procures any other person to place, his spouse in a house of prostitution or compels his spouse to lead a life of prostitution is guilty of pandering and shall be punished (a) Where physical force or the immediate threat of physical force is used upon the spouse, for a category C felony as provided in NRS 193.130. (b) Where no physical force or immediate threat of physical force is used, for a category D felony as provided in NRS 103.130.2. Upon the trial of any offense mentioned in this section, either spouse is a competent witness for or against the other spouse, with or without the other's consent, and may be compelled so to testi201.320 Living from earnings of a prostitute.1.A person who knowingly accepts, receives, or appropriates any money or other valuable thing, without consideration, from the

proceeds of any prostitute, is guilty of a category D felony and s hall be punished as provided in NRS

193.130.01.340. Pandering: Furnishing transportation; penalties

1. A person who knowingly transports or causes to be transported, by any means of conveyance, into, through or across this state or who aids or assists in obtaining such transportation for a person with the intent to induce, persuade, encourage, inveigle, entice or compel that person to become a prostitute or to continue to engage in prostitution is guilty of pandering.

2. A person who is found guilty of pandering:(a) an adult:

    2.1. If physical force of the immediate threat of physical force is used upon the adult, is guilty of a category C felony and shall be punished as provided in NRS 193.130

    2.2. If no physical force or immediate threat of physical force is used upon the adult, is guilty of a category D felony and shall be punished as provided in NRS 193.130.)

    A child:

    2.1. If physical force or the immediate threat of physical force is used upon the child, is guilty of a category B felony and shall be punished by imprisonment in the state prison for a minimum term of not less than two years and a maximum term of not more than 20 years and may be further punished by a fine of not more than $20,000

    2.2. If no physical force or immediate threat of physical force is used upon the child, is guilty of a category B felony and shall be punished by imprisonment in the state prison for a minimum term of not less than 1 year and a maximum term of not more than 10 years and may be further punished by a fine of not more than $10,000.A person who violates subsection 1 may be prosecuted, indicted, tried and convicted in any county or city in or through which he transports or attempts to transport the person.201.354.Engaging in prostitution or solicitation for prostitution: Penalty; exception.1. It is unlawful for any person to engage in prostitution or solicitation therefore, except in a licensed house of prostitution.2. Any person who violates subsection 1 is guilty of a misdemeanor.

201.536 Test for exposure to human immunodeficiency virus required; payment of costs; notification of results of test.

1.Any person who is arrested for a violation of NRS 201.354 must submit to a test, approved by regulation of the state board of health, to detect exposure to the human immunodeficiency virus. If the person is convicted of a violation of NRS 201.354, he shall pay the sum of $100 for the cost of the test.

2.The person performing the test shall immediately transmit the results of the test to the arresting law enforcement agency. If the results of the rest are negative, the agency shall inform the court of that fact. If the results of the test are positive, the agency shall upon receipt:

a. Mail the results by certified mail, return receipt requested, to the person arrested at his last known address and place the return receipt in the agency's file; or

b. If the person arrested is in the custody of the agency, personally deliver the results to him and place an affidavit of service in the agency's file.201.358

Engaging in prostitution or solicitation for prostitution after testing positive for exposure to the human immunodeficiency virus: penalty, definition.

1. A person who: (a) Violates NRS 201.354

(b) Works as a prostitute in a licensed house of prostitution, after testing positive in a test approved by the state board of health for exposure to the human immunodeficiency virus and receiving notice of that fact is guilty of a category B felony and shall be punished by imprisonment in the state prison for a minimum term of not less than 2 ears, and a maximum term of not more than 10 years, or by a fine of not more than $10,000, or by both fine and imprisonment.

201.430. Unlawful advertising of prostitution.

1. It is unlawful for any person engaged in conduct, which is unlawful pursuant to paragraph (b) of subsection 1 of NRS 207.030 (which states it is unlawful to offer or agree to engage in, engage in or aid and abet, any act of prostitution), or any owner, operator, agent or employee of a house of prostitution,

or anyone acting on behalf of any such person, to advertise the unlawful conduct or any house of prostitution:(a) In any public theater, on the public streets of any city or town, or on any public highway; or(b) In any county, city or town where prostitution is prohibited by local ordinance or where licensing of a house of prostitution is prohibited by state statute.

2. It is unlawful for any person knowingly to prepare or print an advertisement concerning a house of prostitution not licensed for that purpose pursuant to NRS 244.345, or conduct which is unlawful pursuant to paragraph (b) of subsection 1 of NRS 207.030, in any county, city or town where prostitution is prohibited by state statute.

3. Inclusion in any display, handbill or publication of the address, location, or telephone number of a house of prostitution or of identification of a means of transportation to such a house, or of directions telling how to obtain any such information, constitutes prima facie evidence of advertising for the purpose of this section.

4. Any person, company, association or corporation violating the provisions of this section shall be punished:

    a. For the first violation within a 3-year period, by imprisonment in the county jail for not more than 6 months, or by a fine of not more than $1,000, or by both fine and the jail time

    b. For a second violation within a 3-year period, by imprisonment in the county jail for not less 30 days nor more than 6 months, and by a fine not less than $250 nor more than $1,000.

For a third or subsequent violation within a 3-year period, by imprisonment in the county jail for 6 months and a fine of not less than $250 nor more than $1,000.

REGULATION AND LICENSING OF BUSINESSES AND OCCUPAULAIONS244.345.Dancing halls, escort services, entertainment by referral services and gambling games or devices; limitation on licensing of houses of prostitution.

1. Every natural person wishing to be employed as an entertainer for an entertainment by referral service and every natural person, firm, association of persons or corporation wishing to engage in the business of conducting a

dance hall, escort service, entertainment by referral service or gambling game or device permitted by law, outside of an incorporated city, must:(a) Make application to the license board of the county in which the employment or business is to be engaged in, for a county license of the kind desired. The application must be in a form prescribed by the regulation of the license board. File the application with the required license fee with the county license collector, as provided in chapter 364 of NRS, who shall present the application to the license board at its next regular meeting.

The board, in counties whose population is less than 400,000, may refer the petition to the sheriff, who shall report upon it at the following regular meeting of the board. In counties whose population is 400,000 or more, the board shall refer the petition to the metropolitan police department. The department shall conduct an investigation relating to the petition and report its findings to the board at the next regular meeting of the board. The board shall at that meeting grant or refuse the license prayed for or enter any other order consistent with its regulations. Any natural person, firm, association of persons or corporation who engages in the employment of any of the businesses mentioned in this section without first having obtained the license fee as provided in this section is guilty of a misdemeanor.8. In a county whose population is 400,000 or more, the license board shall not grant any license to a petitioner for the purpose of operating a house of ill fame or repute or any other business employing any person for the purpose of prostitution.

2.   As used in this section:
(a) "Entertainer for an entertainment by referral service" means a natural person who is sent or referred for a fee to a hotel or motel room, home or other accommodation by an entertainment by referral service for the purpose of entertaining the person located in the hotel or motel room, home or other accommodation) "Entertainment by referral service" means a person or group of persons who send or refer another person to a hotel or motel room, home or other accommodation for a fee in response to a telephone or other request for the purpose of entertaining the person located in the hotel or motel room, home or other accommodation.

CRIMES AND PUNISHMENTS 193.130. Categories and punishments of felonies

1. Except when a person is convicted of a category A felony, and except as otherwise provided by specific statute, a person convicted of a felony shall be sentenced

to a minimum term and a maximum term of imprisonment which must be within the limits prescribed by the applicable statute, unless the statute in force at the time of commission of the felony prescribed a different penalty. The minimum term of imprisonment that may be imposed must not exceed 40 percent of the maximum term imposed.

2.Except as otherwise provided by specific statute, for each felony committed on or after July 1,1995:

a.   A category A felony is a felony for which a sentence of death or imprisonment in the state prison for life with or without the possibility of parole may be imposed, as provided by specific statute.

b.   A category B felony is a felony for which the minimum term of imprisonment in the state prison that be imposed is not less than 1year and the maximum term of imprisonment that may be imposed is not more than 20 years, as provided by specific statute.

c.   A category C felony is a felony for which a court shall sentence a convicted person to imprisonment in the state prison for a minimum term of not less than 1 year and a maximum term of not more than 5 years. In addition to any other penalty, the court may impose a fine of not more than $10,000, unless a greater fine is authorized or required by statute.

d.   A category D felony is a felony for which a court shall sentence a convicted person to imprisonment in the state prison for a minimum term of not less than 1 year and a maximum term of not more than 4 years. In addition to any other penalty, the court may impose a fine of not more than $5,000, unless a greater fine is authorized or required by statute.

CONDUCT OF TRIAL NRS175.301.

Abortion or enticing person for prostitution: Testimony of person upon or with whom offense allegedly committed. Upon a trial for procuring or attempting to procure an abortion, or aiding or assisting therein, or for inveigling, enticing or taking away any person for the purpose pf prostitution, or aiding or assisting therein, the defendant must not be convicted upon the testimony of the person upon or with whom the offense has allegedly been committed, unless:

1.   The testimony of that person is corroborated by other evidence; or

2. The person giving the testimony is, and was at the time the crime is alleged to have taken place, a police officer or deputy sheriff who was performing his duties as such. (22)

APPENDIX B
Survey of Elko County Nevada: 2001

Survey for Study of Prostitution in Nevada:
A survey done in connection with a Doctoral Dissertation by Daniel
Tutty For the International University for Graduate Studies

Disclaimer: Please note that the information collected with this survey is for academic purposes only. None of this information will be used for any political or, legal purpose. All responses will be kept anonymous.

Please place a check mark on the appropriate blank line.

1. Gender: Male ____ Female ____

2. Years of education: 0 to 5____6 to 12____13 or more____

3. Have your biological parents ever been divorced? Yes___No____

4. If your answer to item No. 3 was yes, what was your age at the time of their divorce? 0 to 5____6 to 12____13 to 20____ 21 or more____

5. Marital status: Married___Divorced___Separated___Single (Never Married) ____

6. Number of Children: 0____1____2____3____4 or more____

7. Resident of Elko County Yes____No____

8. Religious Preference: Jewish____Catholic____Protestant____other (specify)____None____

9. Your present age in years: 1 to 20____21 to 30____31 to 40____41 or more____

10. Annual Gross Income (in dollars): 0 to 10,000___10001 to 20,000____20,001 to50, 000____50,001 to100,000___100,001 or more____

The following items concern Prostitution in Nevada. Please place a check mark by the appropriate blank line, or fill in the blank as appropriate.

1. Are you aware that Nevada is the only State in the United States in which Prostitution is legal? Yes___ No___

2. Are you aware of any other places in the world where prostitution is legal? Yes___ No____

3. If your answer to item No.2 was yes, please indicate the place or places on the following blank line. _____

4. How many brothels are there in Elko County? 0–5___ 6 to 10 ___ 11 or more ___

5. Have you ever been inside of a brothel in Elko County? Yes___No___

6. If your answer to item no.5 was yes, have you ever had sexual contact with a prostitute? Yes_____No_____

7. Should prostitution remain legal in Nevada? Yes____No____

8. Should prostitution be legalized in the United States? Yes____ No ____

9. Should prostitution be decriminalized in the United States? Yes___ No ____

10. Should prostitutes be eligible for Social Security benefits? Yes ____ No ____

11. Should prostitutes be allowed to sue their clients for nonpayment for services? Yes____No____

12. Should prostitutes be allowed to unionize? Yes____No___

13. Should brothels be taxed the same as any other private business? Yes___No___

14. Have you ever been inside of a brothel in Nevada? Yes ____ No ____

15. If your answer to item No.14 was yes, have you ever had sexual contact with a Prostitute? Yes ____ No ___

16. Is there a connection between the presence of prostitution in a community and the incidence of violent crime (i.e. murder, rape, assault, robbery, or illegal drug trafficking)? Yes _____ No _____

17. If your answer to item No. 16 was yes, how does the presence of prostitution in a community affect the incidence of violent crime? Increase_____ Decrease_____ No Effect_____

18. Is there a direct connection between prostitution and organized crime? Yes_____No_____

19. Would you knowingly allow a brothel to be located in your neighborhood? Yes_____No_____

20. What is the major reason for the apparent indifference to the presence of brothels in Elko County?
    Lack of awareness_____
    Non-involvement_____
    Live and let live attitude_____
    Don't care_____
    A sense of futility to try and affect a change_____
    Other (please specify)_____

Thank you for your answers.
Daniel Tutty

APPENDIX C

Interview with "Holly"

Disclaimer: All names used in the interviews in this book are fictitious, and in no way refer to any persons alive or dead.

Dan-I want people to see it in a more positive light, you know, "Masters and Johnson."

Holly-Prostitution is one of the ultimate expressions of love.

Dan-For anybody?

Holly-Yes, for anybody, gays, blacks, everyone.

Dan-Born when?

Holly-1977

Dan-You are obviously Caucasian, about 5'7"?

Holly-Yes

Dan-Approximately 127 lbs?

Holly-I'm 140, I'm very muscular. The idea of being fat and sloppy is not good for business.

Dan-Eyes?

Holly-Bright green.

Dan-Hair is obviously black.

Holly-Waist length black

Dan-what part of the country were you born in?

Holly-The Northeast

Dan-Education?

Holly-Graduated head of my class in junior high and ten years of college off and on.

Dan-A sampling degree?

Holly-Actually, I was working on a degree but I would have to step away from it. For many years I was a sexual therapist. I then became a stripper. I kind of went back and forth actually, kind of anti-degree Because I don't like all the steps you have to go through to get one.

Live the AA's and BA's its like, it's mind numbing. And it's expensive to get one.

Dan-Are you married, single, divorced, separated?

Holly-Single.

Dan-any kids?

Holly-Decline to answer.

Dan-No problem. Any histories as you were growing up of any physical, emotional, mental or sexual abuse?

Holly-No.

Dan-Just an average, all American childhood?

Holly-Yep, just a kid.

Dan-Strict parents?

Holly-Yes, very loving, very good, very cool parents. Married for many years. We always had what we needed, they provided for us.

Dan-Any legal history?

Holly-No.

Dan-In the interview process you talked to Mr. Arnold, the owner. When you were interviewing for the job here, how is that done?

Holly-How did I get here? How did I get to Wells?

Dan-No that's a later question, but go ahead, how is it done?

Holly-How it is basically done here is most of the girls call up. They get the number vroom a friend, off the Internet, or from a phone book. And um they well, talk to either the madam or Jeff. They will ask for their name, height, weight, social security, and eyes.

Dan-The basic stuff.

Holly-Priors, if you have any.

Dan-they want to know about priors?

Holly-yea, there is certain house rules that we are linked to in this profession. It can work you. The significant issue is on how, I mean, you can have a record, but it depends on what type of felony you have. So that's something you look at.

Dan-Okay, so then you talk to him, and he invites you to the house, or you just come out, or what?

Holly-He will ask you if you have pictures, Internet picture. If they like it or if they're okay, they invite you out, or some girls just show up. Some girls come from other houses.

Dan-So the process doesn't take that much. Just contact and short interview and I suppose if there is room the house?

Holly-Um huh. That, too.

Dan-Is there like a limit, I mean to houses, as to average size or number?

Holly-No.

Dan-It just depends.

Holly-Its all there, there is such a variety in each house that you walk in to, colors, flavors, it's all there. In every house in this state you will find whatever you want. There are right now, I guess on the floors, I would say there are roughly about 300 girls right now working. If you can't find one out of three hundred...

Dan-none are the same?

Holly-N0.

Dan-That's neat. Just like human kind, there are a variety of persons, a variety of needs and a variety of places, that's cool. So how long have you been in Nevada?

Holly-Three years, in and out of it.

Dan-And why Nevada?

Holly-It's legal. I've made it this far in life without a fucking record, and I tell you that's one of my goals, I don't ever want to go to jail, sure I've seen a few? Whatever. I can deal with that. I always wanted a clean record. I always wanted to go to a job and pass everybody's background check. I don't want to get any file pulled and they don't want to hire me because you have a record of something, of loitering, weird when it goes on your record, it's solicitation, which they use as prostitution subject or suspect? They don't have any proof they think, but it's safer too physically, and I'm in the middle of nowhere, nobody knows where I am.

Dan-Well, Wells, Nevada, is pretty much in the middle of nowhere, that's for sure.

Holly-well, you go to any of the houses except Elko, they are the only downtown houses. They are all in the rural areas, or way out in the fringes, of each town, you know what I mean, like in Carson City, it used to take me twenty minutes to get from Mound House into Carson City. I mean to go somewhere, like to get cigarettes, or go gambling. I used to go pick up a lover from Mound House in Carson City or go gambling. I like to go gambling and I went to get drunk one night.

Dan-Well, you've got to have something to do besides what you do **Holly**-A little outlet.

Dan-I don't doubt it.

Holly-It's rare.

Dan-Average workday, how many hours?

Holly-Ah, how do you define work?

Dan-I mean, well you're seeing customers about 2 in the afternoon, **Holly**-We have to be ready to go on the floor by 1:00 p.m. That's when our day begins. I have to be up by 11 a.m. They come wake us up. I have to get ready. Two hours will easily get someone ready in this house. It's not a problem. We all have it down, too. You know what I'm trying to say.

Dan-Everybody has his or her routine.

Holly-Sure, I have to be ready by 1 p.m. It all depends on how busy the night has been and the day has been. It varies so much. Lately it's been quiet and everyone's been real nice. I've had a good time. Other times it picks up. Like last night, we went to bed early, and then I remember the phone ringing like it never had and it was bedlam in here till 4 A.M. So you never know.

Dan-it could be anything.

Holly-it really could. The average time spent with clientele, working as such on that level could be anywhere from a total of 45 minutes a day to two hours and forty five minutes.

Dan-About 20 minutes a time?

Holly-Usually, more or less. It depends.

Dan-It depends on the customer and what they want?

Holly-Rarely have I, in this particular house, have not done long dates. I did one long date. It was what we call an "all-nighter." It was a hang out session. We talk a little; it was like a slumber party.

Dan-For which you get paid?

Holly-yeah, it was good, it was a fun time, he was a sweet guy. Well, you do pick up some regulars you know some guys are okay. I have no attachments to anybody.

Dan-No, it's a business. How long have you been in the field? How long have you been a sex-worker?

Holly-I've been a sex worker for eight years.

Dan-Why did you become one? What got you interested in the business?

Holly-I've always been intrigued by this industry. I knew about the houses for a long time from strippers and it was like wow, but I never really had the guts to really call when I was younger. I needed a superior support network to be behind this move, and I didn't have that. I wouldn't have been able to find it in my environment where I was playing and I held off.

Dan-Did stripping for a while?

Holly-Did stripping for a while, got out. Completed a psych tech certificate. Did that for a while. Worked in Hospice with aids patients. **Dan**-Cool.

Holly-and that was very cool. It was very rewarding. I did a lot of psych tech work. I also worked in a drug and alcohol rehab as a psych tech. You know, a nurse, psych tech, whatever. It was good. It was good work. The hospice was good, the drug and alcohol was good, but it was like sometimes when I really felt like I have to, you know it's like wow this person has been through so much. It's like when I see them a month later in the gutter, or just walking around later looking tore up. Its like "what happened."

Dan-A waste of effort, in a sense?

Holly-No, I don't think about it as a loss at all. I don't talk about it was a wasted effort. I talk about it like, well human nature, how it was, but I don't, it's like you know if I use that label for that person. I do think that if that person were to see me everyday that person may be different.

Dan-Again, why did you decide to come to Nevada?

Holly-Right, well I dealt with death a long, long time, paid dealing with the drug and alcohol and it just, I wanted to do something else. So I knew I needed instant gratification. You know, but it goes a little further than that, and I figured that out over time. Yeah.

Dan-The usual fee, does that depend upon the person, does that depend upon the service they require? My impression was that it was pretty much straight genital sex with a condom. Is that pretty much the standard procedure?

Holly-Yeah, genital sex says it all. Um, yes and no.

Dan-some guys might want…

Holly-More guys want

Dan-Oral than genital?

Holly-this week has been oral.

Dan-Really.

Holly-Yeah.

Dan-It just goes in cycles?

Holly-It goes in cycles for the guys. All night sex I would chalk up to 70%. I would call blowjobs to 20%. 15%, or the minority, is fetishes and eroticism. On rare occasions there are the fellows who just get too over-stimulated, and there is nothing I can do for them. I mean, I will only go so far. You know what I mean? It depends on the guy.

Dan-Nothing real kinky though? I mean is that a problem?

Holly-Not here, is kinky a problem with myself? No.

Dan-No, what about anal? Is that very much?

Holly-Um, I don't know, I've only been asked twice this summer.

Dan-I mean, some guys, that's their thing.

Holly-Some guys do, some girls do it, and some don't.

Dan-That depends on the person. So really it's just a matter of personal choice

Holly-It really is, um, that's the bottom line. Yea, there's personal choice all around. There's personal choice in walking through those doors. There's personal choice in every person that you take back to the room. There's always personal choice.

Dan-You can be selective, even if you do the line up and they choose you, you can still refuse?

Holly-Absolutely, absolutely.

Dan-If you don't like how he looks or what's going on?

Holly-Yeah, or if you get a bad feeling or this guy looks abusive. You can say you know, you can do what's called a "price walk". Sometimes you don't want to hurt someone's fucking feelings, because, that's not what this business is about.

Dan-Yeah, this isn't about hurting feelings.

Holly-Right, because you may not or one particular girl may not, but then another particular girl will, you know, and you have to kind of figure that out among the women that you live with and know who to go to too.

Dan-What happens to the money?

Holly-The house gets the money. So I get my bills paid, and she gets her bills paid. The baby gets the formula or she pays her tuition, she pays her rent.

Dan-Do you do any kind of inspection of them, I mean physical inspection?

Holly-Of course.

Dan-When does that come in, is that after the "price walk" as you say?

Holly-The price walk that's when you turn somebody away.

Dan-Okay, that's a turn away.

Holly-That's a negative.

Dan-The "price walk" is bad?

Holly-It's not bad.

Dan-it's just you're not going to engage in anything with them.

Holly-A "price walk" is a negative because you're not going to make as much money. You won't make any money. Then you've got to try again with somebody else. You understand?

Dan-Yeah. So let's just say that everything is cool and you say O.K. and this guy is fine and you agree on the price, everything is cool, then you go back to the room, is that when you do the inspection? Does he just get naked right away or what?

Holly-All negotiations take place within your room.

Dan-Okay.

Holly-When they come in and you guys figure out what you're going to do and the price for such activities, or therapy.

Dan-Sex therapist?

Holly-Yes, exactly, exactly.

Dan-Okay.

Holly-That's what I call myself.

Dan-Sex therapist?

Holly-A surrogate.

Dan-Surrogate, yeah surrogate would work.

Dan-Any disease.

Holly-Yeah right, 'cause you can't check for the viruses, you know but you can do other visual checks.

Dan-For physical symptoms.

Holly-Right, I'm there to help prevent the spread of HIV through condom education.

Dan-That is really remarkably effective, given the statistics.

Holly-Yes, it is. If they are used properly.

Dan-Yes.

Holly-A lot of Americans do not know how to use condoms properly. You know, there needs to be some kind of training. They need to be shown how, and we are just the ones to do it. You know, put on a condom, and suck a dick. There you go. When we do the checks I've seen lots of cases of stuff or I've had girls come to me and say, Hey Holly, will you come double check this? Or maybe I've been like unsure and will you please come and check this out?

Dan-Just to make sure?

Holly-Yeah, because it looks like it, but I just want to be, um, you know, it's like, this is my assistant.

Dan-This is my assistant, and she is going to check it too. So lets just say it looks as though something is suspect, well, and then what happens?

Holly-You just...I say, Oh wow, look what you got here, nope, sorry.

Dan-Sorry? Can't do it. Then they are out of there?

Holly-Uh huh, it depends upon who I'm talking to.

Dan-You have to have standards, come on, you have to be fair as well. Oh sure.

Holly-You know what I mean? And also fairer than some, so I'm not going to get a whole bunch of money out of them.

Dan-Okay, now, if you don't want to commit on this next question, you don't have to but, approximate annual income? What does that usually...is that six figures? Does it run to that much?

Holly-It can.

Dan-On average?

Holly-Easily, on average, I would say, not on average, but I would say, the women out here who are smart about it and business minded, and don't have any baggage, you know, uh, stuff to deal with **Dan**-And a good investment portfolio someplace?

Holly-Perhaps, uh, you know, to get to that level.

Dan-Um huh.

Holly-It'd be well, to have to figure out to have those accounting skills upon yourself. And how to market yourself and be your own promoter, accountant.

Dan-Actual dollars, specifically $100,000?

Holly-It can I'd say run between high fives and

Dan-Low eighties, low seventies?

Holly-Low sixes. High fives to low sixes.

Dan-On average?

Holly-Yeah definitely you know, if you do it right.

Dan-Okay

Holly-A professional should do it right.

Dan-That's the whole point; you do it right, don't you?

Holly-Yeah.

Dan-That's why you're doing it, is to do it right.

Holly-The job costs us a lot of money. I mean, we may pull in more than one hundred thirty thousand dollars; I am fixed to write out a good twenty-five more thousand of that just in traveling expenses, living expenses...

Dan-Tools of the trade.

Holly-Right, so personal net profit, I say would be in the high five figures.

Dan-Okay then, of course taxes would be in the 40 percent bracket, is it that high?

Holly-I don't remember.

Dan-When I talked to Mr. Arnold (the owner of the house) he said he was an accountant.

Holly-My personal one wasn't a whole lot last year. It wasn't that high and when I used to make that kind of money as a stripper, you know, you have to take that part out though.

Dan-The IRS (that wasn't Holly-that was a glitch in the tape. That wasn't Holly that was another person who just walked by; I don't know why she said that. We were just talking about the situation with income on average low fives to high sixes?

Holly-I'd say low fives to no, no, no, high fives.

Dan-High fives to mid sixes?

Holly-No, high fives to low sixes.

Dan-Of course, you're aware that Nevada is the only state where prostitution is legalized at the moment.

Holly-Yes.

Dan-Do you favor legalized prostitution in the United States?

Holly-Sure do.

Dan-Why?

Holly-That way I would be able to work in my own town. I would be able to set up a house a business; you know a house with trained women, and in the best business. Yes, and own it. Have it.

Dan-Utilizing your skills that you have from your own experiences. **Holly**-As a communicator.

Dan-And setting up a house.

Holly-Yeah, it takes skill and I know where my market is! You know what I mean, and I know how to advertise it.

Dan-That's the key, knowing your market and how to advertise for it. Making it cash in. Next question, do you feel there is a connection between prostitution and organized crime?

Holly-No.

Dan-Okay, why not?

Holly-Because I am an individual businesswoman, and I am not supposed to be involved in those situations or the house owners discourages that. The women come into the house to develop some strength. You know what I mean. I've seen women get away from bad boyfriends, bad situations, rise up out of poverty, whatever it may be, you know what I mean, and work.

Dan-What about alcohol or drug addiction, does it have a connection to the women in the house?

Holly-Help is very easily attainable here, I mean through this place. I mean there is always a need to be accepted as you are.

Dan-Literally. Do you feel that the presence of legalized prostitution increases or decreases the incidence of physical violence and or violent crime in a community?

Holly-In a community?

Dan-Yeah.

Holly-It decreases it. If it were legal in a community and women who lived in that community could share their experiences the rate would go down dramatically.

Dan-What about women in the business who have a hard time managing their money?

Holly-You are surrounded by women who share the same experiences as you do and can give you advice. One thing I tell women over and over and over again save your money, save your money. Put it away. You know what I mean.

Dan-Have you met any women in the trade who are addicts or drug addicts or alcoholics?

Holly-Sure, they come in all groups of people.

Dan-There is nothing particularly distinctive about working in a house that keeps you from the general law of human nature? Why do you think there is so little opposition to bordellos in operation within a community? Because, in Elko, it's rarely even noticed. It's right downtown, but no one notices that it is there.

Holly-Um

Dan-The reason why I mention this is because my advisor at Wisconsin was shocked at the indifference. I was going to do something else for my project to be honest with you and when talking about it, I mentioned to him about the conditions in Elko and about the houses and stuff, and he was like dumb-founded that there weren't protestors out with signs picketing the front of the place and all kinds of things. So, why do you think the community is apparently indifferent to that whole situation?

Holly-Because they are a tradition I suppose.

Dan-I mean think about it, this house has been in continuous operation here in Wells for 133 years. Well this place has.

Holly-Yeah

Dan-It was here before the railroad tracks were laid. I just don't understand the response of the community?

Holly-Because cat houses, whether people want to admit it or not, contribute a lot of money to city coffers.

Dan-Yes they do.

Holly-You know what I mean, and I don't think were not so well accepted as we are tolerated, you know, but then of course a few of the girls who work at the cat houses are easily met. More people here have more interaction with women who work in these houses, and they see us in our daily life. They see us going to the store, going to the casino, going to the park. We run into certain people around town, so they're just like, oh, and they know, you're not from here; and they see you every so often.

Dan-So they kind of put two and two together and they're O.K.

Holly-Yeah, oh yeah that's one of the working ladies. Hey, um, ya know, she is way cool. You know down to earth.

Dan-I think Nevada in general is just pretty accepting you know. Not prejudicial towards any particular group. Would you agree with that? Holly-Oh, I wouldn't go that far.

Dan-O.K. What would you say?

Holly-I wouldn't go that far. I would go as far as to say that Its not so much that people are accepting as people don't stray from their own game. You can hide in the dessert.

Dan-Yes you can.

Holly-It's very easy to hide out here.

Dan-Let's contrasts this

Holly-Let's just say that we put Donna's House in New York City. **Holly**-Um Huh.

Dan-What would be the reaction? What would be the response?

Holly-There would be a positive reaction if it was done right. O.K. We will legalize you, but here are the laws and ordinances, and you know it could almost go to state controlled to kid of a state run house.

Dan-Would State controlled be good?

Holly-You know what I mean? Because they build the houses you get licensed for it. You work in it.

Dan-Owned by the municipality?

Holly-Sure

Dan-Owned by the state?

Holly-Sure

Dan-Owned by the county?

Holly-Sure

Dan-Owned by the whatever?

Holly-They're city workers who bring in the most money.

Dan-As a category yes. So you wouldn't be opposed necessarily to the idea of state control?

Holly-Almost, I mean, it's an idea or if I went, I mean all right, first off to break the law down you know, to say that I could ever build a house and then advertise for workers to get started you know what I mean?

Dan-My thought would be is that we could do something, you know, or a step in that direction. Whereas it would be under close scrutiny by the government, but still privately owned and privately operated and controlled.

Holly-I think we're scrutinized enough actually, under the eyes of the government.

Dan-Do you think it would ever come to state-run?

Holly-Never, never

Dan-Too independent?

Holly-Can't, can't have the government that deeply involved. Just keep your hand out of my panties. Just get your hands out of my panties.

Dan-Well, you've got to draw a line someplace, I guess.

Holly-There should be more houses. There should be houses with women running them. There should be people running the houses who have been through those doors. People who are aware of the rights I possess and the rituals should run them.

Dan-Have you ever worked the streets?

Holly-Never.

Dan-What do you think about street workers?

Holly-More power to them.

Dan-They seem to be singled out as though, I mean as targets of violence.

Holly-Because they are right there in the street. They don't have anyone protecting them.

Dan-All the more argument then for the bordello. Get them off the street.

Holly-If you want a cheap thrill then go to a house, and get your cheap thrill, a condom will be used. Where you don't have to be afraid of wearing a condom will be used for client and sex-workers protection, you know, on both ends of it.

Dan-Right.

Holly-You know what I mean

Dan-Sure. I think that is one of the major arguments for it. I mean, lets face it, there are too many girls left out there in the street that are getting eat up and wore, and getting STD's, and all kinds of things and it's a horrible place for them.

Holly-Well, if they're going to be street walkers, then they are lucky if they're never going to get hurt or messed with, or addicted to drugs and they are doing it for the thrill. There's a least half of them wind up with an STD. You must use protection always, always, always use protection. That's like my date. I'm always pushing safe sex. I'm for it because that's the law. It's for your protection and for my protection. You know, I pay a lot of money to be in this business. **Dan**-And I don't want to lose it to an STD from you.

Holly-Right, even something that could be cleared up with pills. You know I would never go there and not talk about it. That's' foolish you know. That condom is a barrier.

Dan-It's a separation.

Holly-Totally, totally.

Dan-In Europe, the workers there at least in Germany have been allowed to unionize?

Holly-Yes, the red dress. Unionization, yes, but we would need a lobbyist, in order to be effective. The brothel owners, they have a lobbyist. The working ladies, we don't. Hey, you know, if we had somebody to speak for us, sure. But, do you know how difficult it is for five, six hundred working girls to contribute so much money for this lobbyist, for their rights; and then to get them together and you know, put them into one constituent, in their areas.

Dan-So the concept isn't a bad idea, but the organization of it would be very tough.

Holly-I feel the organization of it would be difficult.

Dan-Do you have the right to sue your clients for non payment of services?

Holly-Yeah, it's a business, small claims court, absolutely.

Dan-There you go.

Holly-Welcome to my house of payment.

Dan-Has is been done to you?

Holly-No, if they do I'll call their wives.

Dan-Better than a small claims court.

Holly-Oh, any day, any day, and I must say you know what, I bet I could talk a wife into paying his debts as well.

Dan-O.K.

Holly-I got a little secret for you.

Dan-What do you think would happen if we were to get legalized prostitution across the United States? What do you think would happen to the number of streetwalkers?

Holly-I think they would go down.

Dan-I would hope so.

Holly-I would think it would disappear.

Dan-If enough houses were established?

Holly-Yes, because they would have some place to sleep, they would have food, they would have protection. They could at least save all their money and take off. You know I have known girls who have had places in town why don't you just pay your rent? It's easier to live here than to rent. You can work or not work. In Nevada, some houses have it where they will help a girl out in several ways.

Dan-Some girls come off the street, get educated, get a career.

Holly-I don't know how a woman would feel about putting herself through college living in a cathouse. I think that would get kind of strange.

Dan-Describe your childhood, which you already have?

Holly-Yeah.

Dan-Good, straight family? Any particular event in you childhood or upbringing that brought you into being a sex worker? Any events in your childhood? Something that you mentioned earlier about curiosity, about when you were a stripper and then you came into the business. Was it like even before that like in your childhood, something that happened, that might have happened that triggered something?

Holly-Um, the only thing I could attribute to it was my parents encouragement of me to read. I read books about women in this country and these women, or a lot of these women were sex workers. They were prostitutes, and very famous women. Their lives were so incredible, so colorful and so rich, and I think that was a lot of it.

Dan-Kind of pointed you to that, and you do smoke?

Holly-Yeah.

Dan-Do you drink alcohol?

Holly-Oh, occasionally.

Dan-But not on duty?

Holly-Definitely not when I'm on the job. Definitely not on the job. I get one night, and that's usually when I lose it. But, that's it. I have guys who ask me a lot would you like a drink, would you like a drink. Personally I'm uncomfortable especially with the people who come here to get laid, especially with the people who come through here. **Dan**-I'm hesitant to ask this question, but have you ever been treated for any mental disorder?

Holly-Have I? No.

Dan-No. What I'm concerned is you know about is some women, maybe you have even encountered them in the business, it seems as though maybe, like if they had a mental disorder, well maybe not a disorder but like nymphomania or something of a sexual nature. **Holly**-Nymphomania is a terrible word.

Dan-It is.

Holly-I don't, to tell you the truth, I don't think there's any such thing as nymphomania. I don't, no, not at all.

Dan-O.K. It's a natural choice then, it's a natural choice made by the persons involved.

Holly-Um, women who know who they are sexually, and how they feel about themselves sexually.

Dan-Plus maybe the fact that the interview process would probably screen out some of those women who were not mentally, well balanced, you would think.

Holly-Yeah but, you know, people who are mentally unbalanced can keep it under wraps, come on.

Dan-So if you were to scratch the surface a little bit, and what you find will surprise you?

Holly-Yes, yes. But that's not to say that it can't be taken serous as well. That I haven't run into women, who aren't on some form of medication,

Dan-Antidepressants?

Holly-And sometimes their demons come out. But, um, I can deal with it. I don't have a real issue with it. I know how to deal with it more. You know there are some women in the house who don't know how to deal with it. That isn't just the ladies but that also includes some of the management. Being able to call it quits for the safety of everybody you know, it's like hey, the management like pays for the expenses, and gets the girl out of town and give her money, and sends her home.

Dan-You are really kind of pointing toward a management career aren't you?

Holly-I can run a house better than a lot of people.

Dan-I think you're being modest. What do you see is the future for prostitution in the United States or in the world? Where do you think it is headed? What do you see, where do you think it's headed? **Holly**-In the United States, we got to get it legalized. If we were the model for bordellos, then a lot of things would cut down like violence, like HIV's. The Dutch, they've already got a grip on it. Germany, they've got a grip on it. I've always wanted to go to Amsterdam and check out the red light district. I would like to go to Amsterdam, and I would like to work for a week. I'm already a whore. I know that much. I would like to learn about this window thing. Yea, I like the window.

Dan-Well, the regulation of course is that can't advertise per se, and a time honored tradition, I mean that's been around for a very long time. But things change, I mean with the new regulations.

Holly-But they don't have to advertise. Everybody knows that stuff has been there for years and years. And in Europe, prostitution is cool. Being a prostitute is more accepted there than we are in America. You know that's all together different.

Dan-Here in Nevada, it seems anyway that they are going toward the all inclusive kind of complex, by putting houses in connection with the resort. Have you heard about that?

Holly-One house. Oh wait, two houses, have done it. Do I think it will work? I think if you're in an area that will support that. In a place that brings in that kind of money. You know you have to count money, and a girl's income as well depends upon the region of the state. You have economic factors in any form of prostitution.

Dan-Vegas, large incomes?

Holly-Well maybe, maybe not, you can make a decent income here, here in the desert, you don't get the gigantic influx of money like in Vegas, there are more high-rollers. But, there's a lot more investors, you got to start on top of your money and watch things, you know um, pay attention to what time of the month it is pay attention to the cycle of the moon, it sounds slightly witch-crafty, but you know.

Dan-Changes in the weather? How does that affect things?

Holly-It affects things a lot. It snows down there.

Dan-True.

Holly-I am a snowbird.

Dan-You get out of here when it snows?

Holly-Um huh.

Dan-So how long do you feel your career is going to be? How long do you feel you will be in the business?

Holly-Three years.

Dan-That's your time frame?

Holly-Three years, that's it. End of the line. I'll get all the information I'll need.

Dan-All the information you need to make it happen?

Holly-Yeah, but, you got to do your research first. You got to put yourself in the trenches. I certainly am.

Dan-Been there, and done that?

Holly-Yeah, I've heard it all, seen it all, and damn near done it all. **Dan**-At least all that you were willing to do anyway.

Holly-Exactly, which is my boundary.

Dan-You've got to have boundaries

Holly-I need to have a partner to help be get things done. I know some women who can totally do it on their own, they're like steam engines, that's awesome, you know, and let them go. Different strokes for different folks. You know, in my job that you do, it s a cooperative thing too, you need a partner. You now I told you I have a partner, a very incredible, intelligent man. He's awesome; you know it just doesn't get any better than that, to have someone who is just great. You know, when it comes to psychology, we are getting a little name as a couple for ourselves around town.

Dan-San Francisco?

Holly-Yes, It's nice. I am fortunate.

Dan-O.K. Is there anything else I should know?

Holly-Do you have any other questions, did you cover everything? **Dan**-It's enough.

Holly-It's nice to relate to people who know what they are talking about. Personal experience, it's there. Observe it for an extended time and then make a judgment. You know it's life, yeah it's a life, but I'm like miles from my home, and if I didn't have to work miles from my home, I would be happier. I would like to set up shop, get some ladies and like go home and you know whatever time I go home, or you know 11 to 7.

Dan-Regular hours?

Holly-Yeah, the lunch crowd and the dinner crowd. You girls, I'll be back and checking on you, I'll be checking on the books at midnight. **Dan**-Yeah, there you go.

Holly-Yeah, 11, 7, and midnight and go home to a bed and you know, a house that runs well. A house of professional women.

Dan-Trust is a big issue here isn't it?

Holly-Trust is a huge issue. Trust is a gigantic issue. You know, you have to either be modern or madam, and have a relationship with the girls like the madams do. I've been there. I got a right to the basic benefits, you could call it a job, granted, I was getting paid a decent wage, but it wasn't enough. I had to work these terrible hours in order to get that decent wage, and what I made in a month, I make in one week. You know what I mean? So there's balances, and being able to recognize that and, first I know when it is better for me, and the other stuff is fine, I can handle it. I can do this. I am way open to my psyche. You know this is an intense business, and like I get up at 11 and my day is on the go.

Dan-What would you change about the industry?

Holly-The industry itself, the collective thought of all the women is to fight for your civil rights. I wish there was even more education in this industry. I mean, we all know about the health checks, we all know how to do the dick checks, you know. I run into a lot of ladies who have boyfriends you, know, they fuck guys on the outside, but they're not using protection, you know what I'm saying. Precaution by measures, that needs to be instilled I have a life partner. I will get in on with one person, but I will use protection, because I don't want my partner to get sick and I don't want my partner like if he decides to sleep with somebody to come home to me with something, do you know what I mean? So you know, condoms, birth control all that stuff, you know, easy access to abortion, you know.

Dan-All the rights?

Holly-Yeah, you know it comes down to everybody in life has their won situation, where its better for them.

Dan-Does a person really know what she wants? That's' not particularly bad.

Holly-Well, the bottom line I say regarding prostitution is fuck poverty, fuck poverty that is the bottom line, when it comes down to it. **Dan**-Economic power translates to social power huh?

Holly-Exactly.

Dan-And social power leads to social change.

Holly-That's correct. Women should have a bigger voice, we have voices, and we've got lots of voices.

Dan-not unified.

Holly-Yeah, we need to have a better voice. He who has the money makes the rules. And I wish they all knew this and they understood it and work with pool and me together and run this country. You know, if I was president. That's not beyond the realm of possibility.

Dan-Think you'll get it?

Holly-Who me? I don't want to get shot!

(Apparently, Holly had presidential aspirations.)

APPENDIX D

Interview with Paula

(I used the letter P for Paula, D for Dan, K for Kathryn, my wife, and G for Glitter)

P-Larry was raised in the South as a gentleman. He has a degree in accounting. He is going to college right now to become take doctor's notes.

D-Medical transcriptionist.

P-Yes, Medical Transcriptionist.

D-Right. To do billing and stuff.

P-Yes, because you see even the school district hires somebody to do this for them. Basically they are getting people that are not billing correctly, and if you bill one time that is incorrect then you cannot come back. Now we are in continuing education. I worked for welfare when I was 21 in Louisiana and loved it. I had my own upholstery business, I have worked in Indian housing building and I worked for Senior Citizens. I went to Ely to run three departments housekeeping, dietary and laundry, so we have been in other businesses.

D-You've been around.

P-People love Larry as well they should.

D-One of my students knows Larry and she works at the library here in Carlin.

P-Yes, he goes to the library. He gives away scholarships to seniors. You can see all these plaques over here; he gives Ms. Borden $500 every year for her project in Elko even though Elko is not here and he gives money to senior citizens. He gives stuff out to Palisades. *(Palisades has a Christmas display for children. They give free stuffed toys to the children. The stuffed toys are given to the prostitutes by their clients who in turn give them to the children for Christmas.)*

D-That's for their Christmas thing.

P-Here is one of our ladies. Would you like to talk to her? This is Glitter. This is Dan Tutty. He is doing a dissertation for his Ph.D. He went over to Geoff Arnold's and talked to a girl there. I told him he could talk to one of our girls.

D-If that's okay.

G-That's okay.

K-I came along because his glasses are broken and he can't drive without them.

P-Well he just wants to ask some questions about the business and you don't have to give your name or anything do you?

D-Oh gosh no.

P-Oh, Okay.

D-Just some general things.

K-Come on. You can sit here. (Gesturing to a place next to her at the bar.)

P-Just questions about the business. I will not call out her name, but she has been with us for 9 years off and on. Of course she goes home for vacations.

D-That's good. Okay, what my paper is on is basically about the idea of Nevada having legalized bordello prostitution, because it's the only place in the U.S. where it is legalized and when I mentioned my topic for my advisor he was kind of stunned by the fact that there isn't more opposition to prostitution in Elko County or basically in Nevada. I told him that it's been an institution for a long, long time and it's been utilized for a number of years since 1972. Basically he went well, gosh, you know that would be a fantastic topic as to why Nevada is that way and more importantly the application that that made to the U.S. as a whole, where we can get some girls off the street perhaps and make them safer, where they'll have more opportunity for health benefits and those kinds of things and will have a beneficial effect on the community in terms of the monies generated from taxes that kind of thing.

P-We (houses of prostitution) pay the highest taxes.

D-Basically I interviewed a young lady in Wells over at Donna's Ranch. I asked how she got into the business, why she came to Nevada and what she saw as the plusses and minuses of working in a house versus working the street.

G-I don't know anything about working in the streets. I never worked in the streets.

D-What about your experiences? You know a lot of the ladies that work in the houses have not worked on the streets.

S-Un huh.

D-You know they just set a standard for themselves and they're not willing compromise that standard in terms where they work or what they will do. One question I asked the worker at Donna's Ranch was what is what her day was like, her hours and such. What she described to me was that she got up about 11:00 in the morning and had to be on the floor at 1:00 P.M. Do you find that is typical for here?

G-No, this house is 24 hours so it's in and out, up and down.

D-Just anytime? Well, that's different then.

P-We don't have line-ups here. We have their (the workers') pictures and nobody comes in unless they've been talked to.

G-Where do you keep the pictures?

P-I have them back there right there next to you. If you men come in here and you have not talked to anybody, then I would show you her pictures and you would pick a girl and I would go get her for you. We don't do line-ups, too sleazy.

D-That is definitely struck me as kind of odd because when I had gone in for the interview (at Donna's Ranch) I was waiting for Mr. Arnold and he had a customer come in while I was waiting and they did a line-up for him.

P-Yes that is because one time a gentlemen came here and he said he'd gone to the Mustang and he didn't know anything about these places and all these girls where coming to him and the last one came in and she was older and she said her name and he didn't want to hear all this again and he picked her and he was so happy when she did that because she taught him what it was all about.

D-I see.

P-People come in and tell you a lot of interesting stories.

D-I would love to hear them. So how long have you been working here? Have you been here for a while?

G-Off and on for 9 years.

D-Why did you become a sex worker? What was the decision that you made when you said I'm going to do that kind of work? Was it the money or what would you say was the main reason why you chose this work?

G-To go to school and because I like sex.

D-That seems to be a major reason that a lot of the girls have. So you like sex and just to support your tuition and that kind of stuff.

G-Um hum. Okay.

D-In terms of your customers, what would you say the trend is as far as what type of things do they like? While I was talking to one girl over at Donna's she was saying that it's pretty much straight genital-to-genital normal sex. I guess the majority of the persons like that.

G-You're not going to believe this, but no, I don't have a lot of sex, not a lot of sex. A lot of guys (we get a lot of driver) who just like to lay down and have a massage.

D-Oh, I see, well that's a good alternative.

K-Do you get a lot of the truckers through here?

P-The truckers are our bread and butter. Not that we don't have locals, but it's not from any of these gold mines because they are checking them first. They don't dope and drink and all that stuff so it's only sub-contractors that are doing things up here, drillers those kind of people.

D-I see. So do you have a regular amount of time you usually work, like say a month or two?

G-No, I get to go home about the end of the month.

D-San Francisco?

G-No, I have lived in Elko, Chicago, California, and in Nevada. I'm a military child so I did a lot of moving around.

K-That's how I grew up, too.

D-Kathryn grew up moving around too, her dad was in the Air Force. So how long have you owned this place?

P-15 years. Yes, we've been open since 1989.

D-What do you think is going to happen as far as the prostitution here in Nevada, do you think it's going to stay small like this with the small houses?

P-I think it's going to die.

D-You thinks it's going to die?

P-Because they will not allow our advertisements. They are not getting the younger girls and the ones that are more mature are going to drop out. It will just die from lack of workers.

D-What kind of time limit are you talking about, one year, two years?

P-I can't predict when, honey.

D-So you think it's on its way out.

P-I feel like it is, because when we first came here we could still advertise in Reno and we got 21 year old girls and they only lasted a couple weeks because they took names and kicked ass while they were here. My daughter is a beautician and she did their hair and got them all fixed up, ready to go and I just say it's not going to last forever, it will simply die. Now, if you go down to Mound House and interview my favorite guy (and his name will come to me) he has a lot of different girls down there.

D-Mound House

P-Yes.

D-Okay, where is Mound House?

P-Carson City. And Larry could come with the answer if he was here. He's on T.V. all the time and that type of thing, and he put out a video and now I'm supposed to have another video. The other one was too bad to watch but this other one should be coming from the gentleman that's supposed to be representing us at the legislation, but he hasn't sent it yet.

D-If you had to give reasons why bordello prostitution should keep on going as a service to a community or whatever, what would be the reasons that you would give? What are the major pluses for us having bordello prostitution?

P-Like I said before, you don't have the rapes, you don't have the molestations that they had before and it brings in a lot of income for the city that they would not get otherwise. So, oh I think it's going to keep going but I've always said it will die from lack of new people coming in, younger.

D-I see.

P-I don't know how young the girls where at Donna's.

D-My impression was that they were probably mid 20's to mid 30's.

P-Thirty?

D-Yes. Normally how many girls do you usually have here?

P-Three to five. There is also Jan, who does our books, helps with the cooking, the housekeeping, the laundry and tending the bar, because you don't know at 6:30 in the morning what customers might drive in here. So somebody has to be on their feet.

D-Ready to greet the customer and take care of business?

P-Yes, and or if he wants a girl, maybe he doesn't, maybe he just wants to have coffee, a shower or a beer, whatever we advertise is available at no cost. We advertise a shower, good conversation, great turn-around parking, iced tea, lemonade or coffee and these things we should give very graciously.

D-Indeed.

P-And if not, you should not advertise them. I still get children in here that I taught school also.

D-They know you as a good person and that's a neat thing. The community really hasn't protested much against your place have they?

P-Never.

D-Why would you say that's true?

P-Well, because Larry is very popular here. He is out backing things, as rightly we should be doing, and because they wanted this here. So why would they suddenly decide to protest us? Even the Mormon church wants us here, honey.

D-That surprises me that the Mormon Church wanted you here. The Mormon church basically, as you said earlier, wanted you here because they felt it would help protect their girls from the influx of workers and stuff from out here.

P-And they knew Larry and me and they knew his wife and they knew we were not going to do something unlawful or something like that. You know in spite of their restrictions, most of those girls by 15 are pregnant.

G-So just check it out one time. Well, if you can't sit down and talk to your children and you're watching them hitting, wasting, crying, then you can't have it and then with this crying, hitting and bruising won't do any good.

K-No it won't.

P-They're out there in that moment of passion, they're going to do what they're going to do.

K-That's right.

P-So I'm not speaking bad about the Mormon Church, but I know that I raised four children by myself, from the time their Father died, sent them to college, I taught days and then I worked nights from 11–7. They had a babysitter and they were in bed, so all the time they were up mother was there. Mommy, as they called me, was sitting right there. I was not some other place, not saying I didn't have dates or that I didn't have friends. I bought a big house up there, we remodeled it and everybody wrote down where they were at, so if anybody needed anybody we knew we could find them.

D-Good idea. In terms of the general impression that you think prostitution has on the rest of the country, what accounts for the general objection that it seems like the rest of the country has against prostitution? Why do they object to that? Is it just because they don't understand it?

P-They're stupid. They don't understand, and I don't want to tell them to go out and do it because it will cut down on our business, but every state should have legal prostitution. Don't think every state doesn't have prostitution because they do. Those girls go to a hotel, they stay inside, the guy knocks on the door, he's made the deal with somebody else, he gives them a chip or something, but they have no protection. They don't know if this guy's a nut or what. Here there's a bar tender out and if there is any problem I tell them the truth. Say you're going to the rest room, get out of the door, come and get me, I will sit down with him, talk it over and two of is going to the door and guess who isn't leaving. I have sat down with them and looked in their beady brown eyes and put on their shoes full of cement and in the end they went out the door happy. There is no sense in sending a man back there because he might like to fight. They are not going fight me, and I tell the girls stay away, don't stand behind me, don't get in front of me, go into the bathroom or another room while I handle this.

D-You take care of it and then they're on their way out the door.

P-Yes they are on they're way out the door. Some of them even ask if they would be allowed to come back in again. And I assure them they would.

D-So the main reason you why you would help somebody out is if say they looked like they where going to cause some problems, like they might get violent?

P-Well, the one guy burned a girl with his cigarette. He is definitely going out and some of them are inebriated and I mean these girls can do what they can do to get them up but they can't do miracles. And if they've taken dope the same way it's not going to work out. So this girl is not a miracle worker. I think they left that one with the blind girl and her person. So they will do what they can do, but if they can't do it, then I'm sorry sir, but that's it, your time is up and we're off and running. Come back another day when you have enough sense not to do it.

D-You can't have both. You can have your drugs or you can have sex but you can't have both.

P-No you can't. It's not my fault and it's not the girl's fault.

D-Of course not. As far as health concerns, the girls are checked every week by the Health Department, or it that who does it?

P-By a doctor who sends it to a lab and if anything comes up bad the Health Department calls here to check it out and the police department comes up and takes their card. In fifteen years we've never had a girls card pulled. And they have an H.I.V. every month and no girl in this business has ever tested positive for H.I.V. If they were to test positive, it would be the first time. See when they come here and they go to the doctor they are tested for H.I.V., Chlamydia, Gonorrhea and Syphilis so if they're going to catch it they'll catch it right then.

D-On the first time.

P-Yes, and the girl will be out. I've never had that to happen.

D-She won't be allowed in the house at all if she tests positive for anything like that.

P-No, no, absolutely not.

D-That's the point I think that really needs to be stressed. When the houses are in operation, they are clean, the girls are safe and the customers are safe.

P-And if you read that when you came in the door, *Condoms Are Mandatory*, they have not been in the past, but probably since we started they have been mandatory. A girl is a fool if she lets some guy, 'course I'm not sitting in there, but if she lets some guy say to her "I'll give you an extra hundred if you don't make me use a condom", she doesn't know what the guy has. The girls check the customers when they wash them up to see if they have any drippings, do they have warts, do they have something like that. If so, they come to me and I go and talk to the customer and tell him that we would just rather not have his business. But I say to the girl, men are very fragile, you sit back here for fifteen minutes and when he comes out he'll sit with his friends and it won't look like we threw him out of the room then.

D-Threw him out of the room?

P-Because, people that don't take care of their health, they know they have something. They don't have the right to pass it on to other people.

D-No, theydon't.

P-I've only had one of those in my fifteen years. So the man is checked. They have a peter pan that they put a little alcohol in and some green soap it and if he has a cut or something and when they yell "wee" we will know it right away.

D-I see. So that prevents that kind of stuff from happening.

P-Yes, we have to protect ourselves you know.

D-Sure, H.I.V. is nothing to be looking at lightly.

P-No, I tell them, six years ago when you tested positive are you going to remember who it is was? No. And for a hundred dollars they catch herpes right off the bat. Herpes are with you forever, but so is H.I.V. You can take medication and never test positive for it, but the medication will run you about $1,500 to $2,000 a month.

D-Yeah, that's expensive.

P-I would say so. How many people do you know that can pay out that kind of money?

D-Nobody.

P-I don't know anybody either.

D-How long do figure you will be able to keep your business open? How long do you plan on running this place?

P-Until we plow it down and drive off.

D-You will be the last owners of this place won't you?

P-Yes we will. It belongs to us free and clear. We put it together in six weeks, which is unheard of and unless I would get somebody that would want a motel situation or a bed and breakfast that might buy it…We could show them how to put it all the way back together the way it was.

D-Well I know a lot of people around Reno and Vegas and those areas that talk about building bigger resorts and you building bigger places and having lots of girls available. Do you think that's going to fly?

P-Well, I can't say. If I could remember the guy's name from Mound House, but if you will give me your card I will send you one of the videos. If you watch T.V. you've seen him on it, he's one of my favorite people, but he no longer, we have called Geoff Arnold that belongs to the association for the simple reason that we went to a meeting and Geoff Arnold allowed this nephew of Susie's to attack John verbally and he handled it very well. But like I said to them this is no way to conduct a meeting, and if you were in charge you would say, "Gentlemen we can discuss this later, we are not going to have name calling in a meeting." That is unacceptable behavior from anybody.

D-Um hum. The association itself, is it strong? Does it really work or is it just kind of a loose sort of group of people that try to meet and go over issues that effect the houses or whatever? Are they an effective lobbying force?

P-It hasn't done shit for us. The guy that lobbies for us, all he ever did for us was to write us to give him money. He knows damn well I don't like him. He tries to bend over backwards right now. But, what you do is somehow, some way, get an update on the laws that they are changing. Like starting October of this year, every girl must register as an independent contractor and must pay $100 a year.

D-They can be taxed.

P-So a man comes here to carpenter, let's say, I don't care who he is, he has to have his certificate to be an independent contractor and they're always try-ing to get these girls for something. Now it's the 1099 that we've sent in so now they know that this girl with whatever social security number she made X amount of dollars. But can they track her down? No. Because the address she gives isn't an actual one. Anyways, honey, that's not my job. That's the police department's job to find out where actually this person lives and you have to fill out this piece of paper I will have Jan fax you one. The police department the first thing they do is run to find out if you have a felony or have any outstanding warrants. If you are a felon you cannot work at this job for five years. And then later the FBI sends me a piece of paper saying if these girls have lied about any arrest they can turn if off.

D-Is each town different for what they require? Do different municipalities have different rules?

P-I don't know I've never been to another town.

D-I'm not sure what the rules are for Wells or if the rules are the same for each town.

K-I would think they would have to be.

P-NRS statutes are what they go by and they're pretty loose as a goose so you can look up the NRS statute about prostitution.

P.-You've got that?

D-Yeah I've got it. In fact I made a copy of most of the NRS statutes. What I'm trying to do is to really present an all-around picture both from an outside perspective looking at it as an industry and also from the inside with the people operating it and from the girls themselves, those that are actually directly involved in the business. Because I think as an overall process it does work and it has in the past. I think that Donna's advertises they've been in continuous operation for 153 years or so.

P-When pigs fly.

D-Well, that's what the guy at Donna's said. But anyway from that point of view you know it's something that works and it works pretty well in terms of it cutting down on crime, the fact that obviously it cuts down on STD's. You don't see any streetwalkers in Elko. You don't see any street people there.

P-Sometimes we get them up at the Pilot (truck stop) but the gentleman that runs the Pilot will run them off. The police could drive up there when I called but if you were in a truck and she was crawling out of a truck, you're not coming back here to testify against her. You're going to drive on to wherever, so they can't really do anything except they usually describe the vehicle. They can run the license to see if they have any warrants and that's the only thing they can do about it. I'll tell you who you should go see, the bailiff, and he was the chief of police over there in Elko and he was going to shut all those places down and he got fired, and now he came back as a bailiff, you know who I'm talking about?

D-No.

P-Larry is good at names. You'll know him, he'll have the unpolished boots. (18)

Appendix E

INTERVIEW AT SUE'S FANTASY CLUB, 475 S. 3rd Street Elko, NV 89801 December 18, 2003, 7:15 p.m. Interview with "Samantha", who is the Operations Manager for this house.

D-Samantha, what is you're position here at the house?

S-Manager.

D-How long have you been doing that?

S-Six months.

D-What brought you here to become the manager of Sue's?

S-An accident (laughing), an accident waiting to happen? No, actually, the owner was looking for someone to do the light bookkeeping. He knew I had the financial background of CPA and the manager he had was not financially literate. So he was looking for someone who was and so he hired me. He asked me if I was looking for a challenge and I'm like why not, here we go.

D-And here you are. How many girls are in the house now?

S-Four in the house right now and one will be back Sunday. I have one that's in Montana she is supposed to be back any minute, any minute for a month now so...

D-So averaging between 5–6 girls?

S-Usually average between 3–5 girls, and that's a good mix.

D-That's a pretty good size, all right, how long has Sue's been in operation? Do you know?

S-Oh my God, 70 plus years?

D-A long time.

S-A long time, all these houses were operating all those years.

D-Wow, do you think it's unusual that these things have stuck around this long right here in downtown Elko?

S-Um, I don't think it's unusual, actually. I think prostitution has been legalized in Nevada for a long time so I think that it's a novelty for people from out of state and I think it's kind of a landmark for Nevada.

D-Do you think Nevada style bordello prostitution or houses of prostitution do you think it would work in other states?

S-Oh yes, easy. I think if you go back and look at the sexual climate in Nevada where prostitution is legal, versus some place like Salt Lake City where there is prostitution is illegal, I think that the crime rate would be dramatically different. I think that is because everybody has their own thing, different strokes for different folks. I think in here you can get anything you want pretty much as far as sex. If they are willing to pay for it, if it is legal and they want to pay for it, the girls are clean, they are not out on the street going after innocent people.

D-I've done interviews at other houses and it's the universal thought that it here it's controlled and it's clean.

S-The state makes a lot of money from it.

D-The state makes a lot of money, I don't know how much…

S-The city makes a lot of money; the county makes a lot of money.

D-I don't know how much money Sue's kicks in, but I'm sure it's a significant amount of change.

S-Yeah, I mean all of them take one heck of a chunk every year. I mean you've got a brothel license, which you've got to renew every year.

D.-How much is that usually?

S-Our license is $2,500 a year, but we pay half, every six months. And we have to have a bar and a liquor license, plus we have to have a normal business license. We have a spa so we have to have a spa permit. We have a kitchen so we have to have a health permit.

D-It sounds like it is all regulated.

S-Yes, it's all regulated and then on top of that we have to pay sales tax on all the liquor that we sell and any merchandise like cigarettes. We don't sell many cigarettes, but like T-Shirts and souvenir stuff we have to pay taxes on them. The State is making out like a bandit.

D-So they don't want you guys to shut down soon do they?

S-You know I really don't understand the thinking of the State because they are making an awful lot of money off the brothels. If you look at the big brothels down there in southern Nevada outside of Vegas, those guys are making a ton of cash. But they have "corner queens" there and they are much more obvious because Vegas is much more in your face, literally right there, more than they are here in Elko. They want our money, no doubt about that because if I'm one minute late paying the brothel license they'll jerk it out from under us. But then we're not allowed to advertise. We are not allowed to advertise in town and we are not allowed to advertise in the phone book as a brothel. We are allowed to advertise as a bar or a club. That's the way we are allowed to advertise in the phone book. The only thing the State has not been able to regulate so far has been the Internet and they can't do anything. So we have a web site and it has pictures of the girls, but that's the only place. It's a little difficult when you're trying to target a certain population and market (you know I mean). We've got lots and lots of guys traveling through on I-80 traveling from Salt Lake to Reno and then coming in from Salt Lake going out to the mines. Heavy equipment salesmen people, Fire Science Academy, we get a lot of guys from there. We have guys from all over the world.

D-Typical month, how many customers through here a month?

S-Per month? Oh Lord, how many guys just coming through the house? Talking a couple hundred a least. As far as gentlemen that come in to party with the ladies it's hard to say. One month we might have 50 and the next month we might have 100. Like one of my girls last weekend had a $1,800 night. At least that was what she booked. What she did is partied with one gentleman all night long. So it's hard to you know…

D-The prices really vary a lot don't they? I mean according to what the guy wants and what the ladies are willing to do.

S-What the ladies are willing to do, how long he wants to party with the lady and according to what his sexual preferences are. So if it's the more kinky stuff he wants, it's going to cost him. The price goes up, and the longer he wants to party the price goes up. Normally it starts at about 15 minutes, which is really the normal you know "in and out" kind of thing.

D-Just a straight kind of party, what are we talking, a couple hundred dollars probably?

S-Most of the time guys can get a straight lay in 10 minutes for a $100.00, that's about par for the course. Bartenders are not allowed to give prices. It's against the law because the girls are independent contractors.

D-So they can pretty much negotiate their own price.

S-They negotiate their own price. Most of the girls are pretty close in price as far as what sort of things they do. It's just that some girls are willing to do some things those other ladies won't.

D-Choices are there from the start.

S-And it's pretty much a house of negotiations. A girl can book a party in the middle of the night that could be $300.00-$500.00 easily. A girl comes out and says I'm going to give this guy 50 minutes for $250.00. What she did is she took $250.00 of that money and stuffed it in her pocket and she's trying to pay the house $250, and she gets half of that $250.00 again. So it's no, no, no, and if you've got good bartender's they'll catch that and say no, no, no you go back and renegotiate with that guy because we are not taking $250.00 for 50 minutes. That's bogus.

D-So it's not that it's what service is provided for the client.

S-Right, Some are pretty good about it and the amount of time that a gentlemen might need and...

D-So how is that done? I mean to the say a guy picks out a lady that he wants to party with and then they go back to the room to negotiate the price? Is that where it's done?

S-Right, normally if a gentleman has never been in a house before they'll have a line up and all the girls will come out, whatever girls you have, and they'll introduce themselves to him. If she's a lady that interests him then she'll take him on a tour of the house. They have a hot tub room, they have a shower, they have a bed, and we have a V.I.P suite upstairs. It's a nice big room with a TV, V.C.R.'s and a lot of mirrors. So she'll show him the amenities we have and then she'll take him back to her room and then he tells her what he's interested in. She gives him the price.

D-Is payment made at that time?

S-Payment is made at that time. If he decides he wants to party with her he will hand her the money or a credit card. You know, however he's going to pay. She brings it out to the bartender and the bartender logs it.

D-At the time when it started and the amount.

S-Right, the bartender will log like how much the party is for, how many minutes the girl is giving him. I have to know so I can do all my paperwork. So I want to know how much the girl's getting and how much the house is getting, because they pay room and board every day and so there's her room and board. She's going to get this much, the house is going to get that much and I want to total off. I want a daily total. I want to know how much all together the girls did. I want to know much each individual girl did and I want to know how much was cash and how much was credit cards. I want to know how many minutes the girls are booking at what amount, because that's really tough trying to find out. If they are trying to rip the house off that's where you're going to see it is right there.

D-So what is a typical night like from 6:00 A.M. to 6:00 P.M.?

S-We open at about 3:00 in the afternoon and close at 3:00 in the morning. You know it just depends on how busy it is. If we still have customers in at 3:00 A.M. we're not closing. Last Saturday night the house next door closed and the house around the corner didn't have a bartender so they weren't serving any liquor and so we were just like getting all these people. We stayed open until 7:30 the next morning. I'm like as long as they are coming in I'm not shutting the house.

D-Had an awesome night huh?

S-Wow, we had an awesome night that night; we had a great time too. D-You usually close at 4 A.M. and then that's it, that's your typical day. You're not a 24-hour house.

S-No, it just doesn't justify paying some lady to come in and work those extra hours. Then I bartend about 4–5 hours a day, trying to keep costs down because I'm salaried. We can save money; it's just like having a regular house. You have to pay utilities, you got to pay your phone bills, go buy groceries, but in this house you got to buy liquor, lots of liquor and beer for sure, and the girls are all, "I need a beer, I need new stereo." I mean you are just constantly going, "ahh."

D-Do you have a regular cook then that cooks the meals for them?

S-No, normally either the manager or me will cook. Sometimes I'll cook something simple; I'm kind of lazy about it. Usually the night bartender, whoever the night bartender is that comes on after me, is usually the one that cooks for the girls and most of the time the girls are like starving to death and they are like can we please have…you know and then I'll cook it early. Normally the night bartender cooks. In the bigger houses they do have actual cooks, though. That's all they do is come in and cook.

D-Someplace like Vegas or Reno, or in the big houses? In the big houses typically how many girls would work in the big houses?

S-Anywhere from 15–40.

D-Wow! That's quiet a few.

S-That's quiet a few. The last I heard the Wild Horse Resort which is over by Fernley, between Fernley and Reno, one of our girls left here thinking that it would be better over there being in a bigger house. She went over there, there were 40 girls and they were all younger than she was.

D-Average age?

S-I would say late 20's early 30's are probably an average age. You've got some that are younger and a few that are older. I've had several girls in here that where 52 and still doing their thing.

D-Still doing their thing. Yeah, in this business I suppose it's pretty critical as far as…

S-You know, but I see that Dan, in my mind like girls that are 52 years old and still prostituting are the ones that have either severe drug problems, gambling problems, alcohol problems, and they can't break out of that cycle because they can't save their money long enough to get help. We had a black lady in here who has been in here off and on for years. She must never have enough money. She went across the street worked over there for a couple weeks and she lost all her money over there. She has such a terrible alcohol and gambling problem that she can't get her life straight. She just lives to pay the house back. That's all she does, it is really sad.

D-What percentage of the girls are alcoholics, relatively small?

S-Wrong. I'd say the percentage would be large.

D-That's usually one of their downfalls?

S-Yeah, well, good grief, I mean customers come to the bar.

They (the girls) come out, the customer will pick her out and maybe he'll go back to talk with her and maybe he's not ready to party quite yet, so he'll say well, let's go to the bar and I'll buy you a drink. So then you have ten customers coming through the house that night that pick you and want to take you back to the bar for a drink. That's ten alcoholic drinks and you do that every night, night after night. Because we are open seven days a week. I mean there you go.

D-What is a typical working day? Let's say a girl that's of average popularity, not a superstar or anything like that, but just an average girl, how many customers, or parties, do you think she'll book?

S-Well, like that one girl I was telling you about Friday night, she had one customer (I forgot she had two customers) and booked $1,800.

D-But typically how much?

S-Typically 4 to 5 parties a day. You don't see girls book a whole lot of parties. I've never seen a girl do one after another after another.

D-It's not like a factory kind of thing.

S-You don't see them doing that kind of stuff. They get sore, they get tired, and it's very stressful for them, it really is. Because you are constantly like smiling and being a nice person and a guy's like got his grubbies on. He's been working on his truck and he stinks and she still has to be nice to him.

D-Do you have them shower up or anything?

S-We offer a shower and if they're really grubby the girl might go, "Please would you mind taking a shower?"

D-What if some guy comes in and obviously he's kind of a risk, looks like he might be a violent person, maybe he's already intoxicated or…S-We have some (guys) come in that are already extremely intoxicated and most of the time the girls won't deal with them at all. They won't even come out for the line up because he's too drunk for sex and they don't want to deal with that. If a guy is rude to the girls at the bar, I don't allow it, because you got to be nice to the girls and show them respect. And if you can't, then there is the door, we don't need your business.

D-Do you check them for like sexual diseases?

S-The girls do.

D-When they take them back for the party?

S-Right. When you take them back for the party that's the first thing the girls do. They always do a dick check. They usually wash them and they have a peter pan. They put warm water and soap in it and wash them and check them out and do a dick check and if they like have any type of sores or oozing or anything like that the girls won't touch them. It is just too risky to take a chance on picking up something.

D-Diseases like herpes.

S-They'll come back out and say, "Sorry. I can't do this go on and give him back his money."

D-Do you throw them out then?

S-I don't throw them out, 'cause they didn't get what they paid for. There are probably houses out there that are not cool about it. It's like you paid for it, too bad you look like you have gonorrhea or syphilis, because the girl isn't going to party with you. Too bad you already paid your money; get out. I don't work that way because I believe that if you treat the customers badly they aren't going to come back and they'll tell all their friends, "They don't treat you right, they screw you around on time," or whatever, so I would just rather give them their money back and say, "I'm sorry, but due to what the lady saw before the party she declines to party with you."

D-So they get angry but not totally, because they don't want anybody knowing what they have.

S-Most often they will not return anyway. If the customer is ungratified I'll bring them into the lounge and say, "Look, you're unhappy. Tell me why you're unhappy. Do you think she shorted you on time or she didn't give you what you wanted or what you agreed to?" You know, tell me these issues. But an older guy would pay like $150 for a party and you still had a little bit of a party. And I gave him the $100 back and kept the $50 because he still did have a little bit of a party and he goes, "That's fair, yeah, that's cool." And they are happy when they walk out and you think he'll be back.

D-In your house are the majority of the customers businessmen. Are they conventioneers, are they truck drivers? What are the majority of men?

S-In our house most customers are businessmen traveling through, Salt Lake people, sales people to the mines.

D-So you don't have many truck drivers?

S-No, because we are in a residential area so the trucks are not allowed to come down here. They could park behind the Stockmen's there in that empty lot, but then they've either got to walk down here or take a cab down here or whatever so truck drivers just are not any part of the business really. We get a lot of guys from Casino Express. I mean last week it was a bunch of guys from Duluth, Minnesota, and they were a kick let me tell you. We had so much fun with those guys. It was crazy. Because it's not legal in the state of Minnesota so you know they had to come check it out.

D-Just to say they'd been in a house.

S-Yeah, just to say they'd been in a brothel. And these were just kids.

D-Do you belong to the Brothel Owners Association?

S-I'm not sure if Jim belongs or not. I think we should be, but I know for some reason the owner Jim has some problem with it and I'm not quite sure what it is.

D-I have that feeling as well. I talked to Geoff Arnold who owns Donna's. He's the president of the Association. And he seems to be all for it. Then I talked to Paula over at Samantha's Place and according to Larry and her it's not working.

S-I know he has some issue with the Association. But he never has told me why. I have a lot of respect for Geoff and Geoff has bent over backwards to help me because he knew I had never been around the business and had no clue what the hell I was doing. Any questions you have, call me. I've called him several times. He's just been great. I had three girls show up from Salt Lake City begging me for three solid weeks to come out and work. I finally let them come out; they come out and it's like well we don't have money to go to the doctor. They have to pay that first before they can work, so I paid for them to go to the doctor. They came back from the doctor and asked, "Where's the quickest place to tan?" I said at Tropical Tan and Tone. We didn't see them again. They went to Donna's in Well's, so I called Geoff and told him what happened. Two days later I had a check in the mail for the entire amount.

D-It's pretty decent.

S-It is decent. I mean he's asked me a couple of times to help him. He had a girl come to town and she had a really bad cold but she only had enough money to pay for her doctor visit and she needed another $35.00 for antibiotics. She didn't have that extra $35.00. Geoff called me and said I'll get you a check in the mail today.

D-So it's just business with Geoff. I mean my impression is he is a businessman and this is a business, fair and simple.

S-He's a CPA by profession so…Well he was the CPA for the brothel for years. There are a lot of things legally they give you. When I first took over they gave me a list of all the rules and regulations. I called Geoff and asked what I could do. He knows about the houses and who owned them originally and what the Madams were like back then. Back then the Madams ran them and Geoff can tell you some terrific stories about it.

D-Do you have so many girls that you don't know them?

S-Everyone of them has their own personality. In the houses it's called drama and every girl has her own thing.

D-So your tempted to say, "Just grow up."

S-I had one, she makes excellent money, she's excellent in the business, she's gorgeous and she's into jewelry big time. I have to actually take her money away from her and put in the safe where she can't touch it. Otherwise it would all get spent on jewelry, diamonds and gold and silver.

D-Better save your money, girl.

S-Well, I think now she's saving it because she wants a breast implant.

D-I guess to each his own.

S-Booking as many parties and she does I don't see why she needs that done. I said, "Like as long as you're booking there is no reason why you need to spend $3,000. The guys don't care."

D-That's really not what they are buying you for.

S-Exactly. God, you can't convince her of that.

D-Well, it's all in self-image I guess.

S-When Sue first came here she was very, very timid and shy. Her self-confidence was not only lacking it just wasn't there, and now she has completely changed. She is Queen of the House now. She is cleaning up; she is respected now. You will find in most houses whichever girl is the high booker in the house is the Queen. They'll come to me and say, "Can I have $50 so I can go to Wal-Mart and get supplies?" I answer, "How long will you be gone?" They reply, "I'll be gone for about an hour and a half." Three hours later they call you from Stockman's and you ask where they are. They tell me they are at Stockman's. When I ask what they are doing there, they answer that they are just having a few drinks and gambling and are broke because they have already lost all their money in the slot machine.

D-So then they get to repay the house that 50 bucks.

S-Yes. I'm not a bank.

D-A day for a girl starts when?

S-Normally they are up by about 2 o'clock in the afternoon. They get up, make themselves something to eat and clean their room. If they need to run errands, they'll go. There is a 5:00 P.M. curfew for the girls. Business is usually good from 3:00 P.M. until around 8:00 P.M. Our best business doesn't pick up until 9:00 to 9:30 P.M.

D-You guys stay pretty steady then until till about 4:00 in the morning.

S-If business is slow we close the house at 3:00 A.M. There is really no reason in keeping the girls up when there is no business.

D-I won't be too much longer I just wanted to get a sense of a typical day here.

S-Some girls are really ambitious and as soon as they hear the doorbell they are right there at the door to look and see who is in the parlor. Other girls are quiet. I've seen the girls who work hard are the ones that are up in the door looking to see who's in the parlor and asking if there will be a line up. They are the ones that are going to make money.

D-What about the girls who don't work as hard?

S-They might make the line up and they might not. They might make $200 a night. The ones that want to work will make possibly three times as much. You know if you are in your room watching T.V. and not being bothered, you won't make anything.

D-What's good for them is good for the house, too.

S-Right.

D-Yeah, well a lot of it is just the attitude of the girls.

S-A lot of times the guys have a hard time picking a girl from the lineup because they are nervous. I see the girls standing in the lineup, looking like they are in the Miss America pageant. They are all standing there and they are all beautiful. The guys are wondering who is going to be Miss America for them and meanwhile their friend is standing there encouraging them to go "do it." They'll just pick any girl and then it's over. Some of the girls who are not picked out in the lineup, but are willing to come back out and sit at the bar and visit with the guys will still book a party.

D-Are some guys very nervous about having a lineup?

S-Yes, some are. I think the lineup is kind of degrading for the girls. I think most girls would rather come out of their room when they know someone wants them for a party rather than be in a lineup.

D-Do the customers feel pressured to make a choice from the lineup?

S-Yes, the guys would rather not have a lineup. It is much more relaxed.

D-Some of the other houses seem to run a little different in terms of style and philosophy.

S-Well you know they used to be run by madams who had first had to be working girls. Take me, for instance. I could never be a madam. I can only be a manager of a house since I was never a working girl.

D-So you're not a madam?

S-No I'm not a madam. I was never a working girl. I've never been in the nude business or industry. I'm a bookkeeper by trade. I've found that in this house there were a lot of things that have been done certain ways forever, because the house was making lots of money. There were lots of customers and things where booming in the town so it didn't matter that they were paying $300 a month for cable T.V. We don't have that luxury anymore. We are saving over $200 a month by going to satellite T.V.

D-What do you think is the future for the houses?

S-I think eventually they'll go away. I don't think that other states will ever legalize prostitution.

D-Why is that?

S-Because of the morality of it. Especially like in the Bible Belt, like the southern states, they will never allow it to become legalized. I think because of the popularity of strip clubs, and strip bars or whatever that eventually brothels will just fade away. I don't think the state will ever shut down the houses. They'll just die out. A comparison of business today versus years ago shows how much business has fallen off.

D-Falling off pretty quickly.

S-Yes. For example a gentlemen who comes through every couple months to sell clothes to the working girls says he believes that probably within ten years the houses will be gone. There is so much sexual material on the Internet that I think the brothels have lost their importance in society. With the Internet I think it's the biggest thing

D-They don't have the draw that they used to.

S-No. It's a novelty, because with so many people traveling through on I-80, they know that it's legal and they have to check it out to see what it looks like. They can go home and tell their friends they were in a brothel.

D-And a novelty is not enough to keep it going.

S-No, it is like those guys from Duluth who traveled here on the Casino Express. They came in just to check it out.

D-They weren't interested in the girls to party or anything.

S-They just wanted to come in.

D-So they could say they'd been in a brothel.

S-Drink at the bar, talk and chat have a good time, laughing and that was it. Not one of them booked a party.

D-So that doesn't make any money then.

S-The bar made some money. We make decent money on the bar as far as our profit on the liquor and stuff, but it's not our bread and butter. That's not why we are actually here.

D-And that's not the purpose of the house.

S-The girls that work the floor make money for the house.

D-It will be a sad day when the houses close for good.

S-I think it will be, too. Because I think a part of history will have died. It's like the Mustang (Ranch). It's a part of history that has died

D-It is sad because it has been such a traditional thing for so long. It's almost like a remnant of the old West. I think that we are running out of time. I want to thank you.

S-Well, you are very welcome, Dan. I hope it helps you.

D-I'm sure it will. (31)

APPENDIX F

Menu of Services, Sharon's Bar and Brothel

978-0-595-37685-8
0-595-37685-1

www.ingramcontent.com/pod-product-compliance
Lightning Source LLC
Chambersburg PA
CBHW051410280526
45785CB00003B/1020